CONTENTS AND ADDRESSES OF HUNGARIAN ARCHIVES

with supplementary material for research on German ancestors from Hungary

Second, annotated edition

Edward Reimer Brandt

CLEARFIELD

Copyright © 1993 by Edward Reimer Brandt
Minneapolis, Minnesota
All Rights Reserved.

Second Edition 1993

Printed for
Clearfield Company, Inc. by
Genealogical Publishing Co., Inc.
Baltimore, Maryland
1993

Reprinted for
Clearfield Company, Inc. by
Genealogical Publishing Co., Inc.
Baltimore, Maryland
1995, 1998, 2002

International Standard Book Number: 0-8063-4607-8

Made in the United States of America

TABLE OF CONTENTS

	Page
PREFACE TO THE SECOND PRINTING	3
PREFACE TO THE SECOND EDITION	4
REVISED INTRODUCTION	6

PART I: OVERVIEW OF GENEALOGICAL RECORDS AVAILABLE IN HUNGARIAN ARCHIVES 18

- A. Key Dates in Hungarian History for Purposes of Archival Research 19
- B. General Description of the Contents of Regional Archives, with Pertinent Historical and Governmental Background Information 20
- C. Description of the Contents and Organization of the Hungarian National Archives 25
- D. Archival Records of Particular Genealogical Value, According to the LDS Family History Library 32
- E. Current Information Regarding Genealogical Research in Hungary 34

PART II: ADDRESSES OF HUNGARIAN ARCHIVES AS OF JANUARY 1992, TOGETHER WITH NOTATIONS CONCERNING SELECTED HOLDINGS OF INDIVIDUAL ARCHIVES 39

- A. National Archives 40
  1. Central Ministry Responsible for Archival Administration 40
  2. General Archives 40
  3. Specialized Archives 41

- B. Local Archives 42
  1. City Archives 42
  2. County Archives 42

- C. Archives in Public and Private Institutions 49
  1. University Archives 50
  2. Academies, Scholarly Societies and Specialized Institutes 50

- D. Religious Archives 51
  1. The Roman Catholic Church 51
  2. The Reformed (Calvinist) Church 55
  3. The Evangelical (Lutheran) Church 57
  4. Other Churches 58
  5. Jewish Archives 59

APPENDICES, TABLES AND MAPS.................................. 60

    Appendix 1: Names of Selected Places in Pre-Trianon
        Hungary in Hungarian, German and Other Languages..... 61

    Appendix 2: Dateline of Historic Events in Hungary
        of Particular Relevance for Research on German
        Ancestors.. 65

    Appendix 3: Select Bibliography of Books and Other
        Materials Useful for Researching German Ancestors
        from Hungary... 74

    Table 1: Number of Native German-Speakers in Pre-1914
        Hungary, by Regions as Defined by Winkler, in Order
        of Such Population in 1910........................... 79

    Table 2: Hungarian Counties and Cities with More than
        20,000 Native German-Speakers in 1910................ 81

    Map 1: Hungary Before and After World War I.............. 83

    Map 2: Hungary: Current Counties and Larger Communities
        (showing concentrations of German-speakers).......... 84

    Map 3: Hungarian Counties Before World War I.............85

PREFACE TO THE 2ND PRINTING (1995)

Only minor changes have been made in this book since the 2nd edition was first published in 1993, so calling it the 3rd edition is not warranted. It has been updated to reflect the current status of publications and of genealogical organizations which are relevant for Hungarian genealogical research. The names of some professional genealogists and translators with pertinent specialization have been added. A few bibliographical changes have been made.

Various spelling or typographical errors, mostly relating to Hungarian diacritical marks, have been corrected. I thank Douglas P. Holmes of the Hungarian/American Friendship Society for calling most of these to my attention and sending me the needed corrections.

                                        Edward Reimer Brandt
                                        13 - 27th Ave. S.E.
                                        Minneapolis, MN 55414-3101

PREFACE TO THE SECOND EDITION

Most of this book has been rewritten for the second edition, with numerous minor corrections and revisions, as well as some reorganization of the material.

The most significant substantive difference between the two editions, however, is the fact that the second edition includes information about the contents of each individual archive which was listed in the *Guide to the Archives of Hungary*, edited by Dr. Péter Balázs (Budapest: Archival Board of the Ministry of Culture, 1976), instead of only the general descriptions for the national and regional archives. This is particularly significant with respect to the regional and the religious archives.

Obviously, I have selected only a small amount of information from the description of holdings contained in the 1976 book. I do not claim consistency in the presentation, partly because the information on the various archives was not of a fully parallel nature in the original source, but mostly because it would have taken a great deal more time to develop a checklist of items and scan the data on each archive for matching information. Nevertheless, I have used certain general criteria for choosing the items mentioned in this book.

First of all, this started out as being a source of information intended particularly for genealogists. Hence, I have sought to maximize the inclusion of information which would be of genealogical benefit.

Of course, in many cases it is uncertain whether certain kinds of records actually contain names or only statistical data, accounts or descriptive material. Moreover, a lot of the information which has been included will be of genealogical value to only a relatively small number of people (e.g., court and orphans' records).

I have paid particular attention to any information which might indicate that Hungarian archives contain information on areas formerly, but no longer, a part of Hungary, as well as the reverse: records on Hungary to be found in other countries. I have also picked up information relating to minority groups, wherever possible. Thus this book is meant to be of as much value as possible, given the sources of information, to everyone who is researching ancestors from what is now, or once was, Hungary.

Second, I have included some historical material, particularly as it might relate to religious institutions (which were the principal source of genealogical information until 1895, even though the post-1828 data is also in public archives now) or to the socio-economic history of the populace. I have minimized references to the kind of political history which tends to dominate most textbooks.

Instead of simply reproducing the descriptive material on the general archives and regional archives, I have rewritten most of it, deleting or abbreviating material unlikely to be of interest to North American researchers and adding clarifying information where I could. Of course, if there are any errors in these "clarifications," I alone am responsible. The terms used in the 1976 *Guide* are not always clear in their meaning, but it would have taken a tremendous amount of time to make sure that my interpretation of archaic terms, technical archival language, and general terms with broad or varied meanings was always precise and accurate. In some cases, I have chosen to use the original words or phrases because of uncertainty as to exactly what they were meant to convey.

I hope that the book will be of value to researchers who are not necessarily interested in genealogy or those aspects of history which I have stressed, because the relatively detailed descriptions in Part I are more or less comparable to the *Guide* in terms of comprehensiveness, even though the descriptions of the holdings of individual archives are not.

A second major change is the addition of a new appendix which lists the Hungarian, German and current names of a selected number of localities which were in Hungary before World War I, with emphasis on those where there were German settlements.

Any corrections, amplifications and suggestions regarding the contents of this book will be gratefully received.

I should alert readers to the fact that the letter "ß" is not a "b," but what is called an "es-zet" in German. In earlier days it was written "sz"; today "ss" is considered the correct rendering. It should be noted that "sz" was in use longer in the German settlements in Eastern Europe than in Germany itself. Thus one may well find a descendant of a German immigrant from Eastern Europe still spelling his or her name in English as "Grosz," for example, whereas this is less likely for those whose ancestors came from the Germanic heartland in Central Europe. The "ß" was used at the end of many words, or at the end of roots of compound words.

As a postcript, I might mention that I generally use my mother's maiden name as my middle name, as was customary in the community where I grew up, in writing for publication, even though my birth certificate records me only as "Edward R. Brandt." The equal, though not identical, contribution of the two sexes to the history of humankind is obvious to any genealogist. I fully appreciate and honor that simple but basic fact.

Edward Reimer Brandt

REVISED INTRODUCTION

How This Book Came to Be:

First of all, my ancestors, my mother-in-law's ancestors and my father-in-law's ancestors all followed different patterns of migration from Western Europe to Eastern Europe, from where they came to North America, mostly Canada. They had remained German in language and culture throughout the several generations they had lived in the Slavic East, before crossing the Atlantic between 1874 and 1907.

Secondly, I became involved with genealogy, at first as a dabbler, despite having learned very little about my European ancestors before adulthood. The incidental identification of my mother-in-law's ancestors who emigrated to Galicia in the 1780s instantly turned me into a serious genealogist. The reason I say "incidental" is that on a visit to Vienna in 1966 I arrived early at the destination where all the family members were supposed to meet, turned around to see the Austrian National Library behind me and went in to browse through the card index. What I found was a gold mine!

Thirdly, I have learned a great deal from the many genealogical and historical organizations (most of them concerned with the history and genealogy of German-speaking ancestors, but not necessarily from Germany) which I have joined since the late 1970s.

The German Interest Group, a branch of the Minnesota Genealogical Society, whose Research Committee I chaired for several years after my return from my third period of work in Europe in 1987, has been an especially important influence. It has now changed its name to the Germanic Genealogy Society, partly because of my insistence that what our ancestors had in common was the German language and, to some extent, a shared culture, not a common point of origin or identification with a single country.

The American Historical Society of Germans from Russia, to whose *Journal* I have contributed on several occasions, provided me with my first opportunity to address a national convention on my genealogical research in Germany. The North Star Chapter newsletter printed my first article on Germans in Eastern Europe.

Two editions of the guide to genealogical research on Germans in the East, put out by the *Arbeitsgemeinschaft ostdeutscher Familienforscher* (popularly referred to by its acronym, AGoFF) served as a most valuable resource. The second edition has been translated and was published in English in 1984 under the title, *Genealogical Guide to German Ancestors from East Germany and Eastern Europe*. The third edition of what is popularly known as the *AGoFF-Wegweiser* (1991) is available only in German.

In 1989 I attended a seminar on Advanced German Genealogy offered by Larry O. Jensen at Brigham Young University and subsequently passed the Family History Library examination to become an accredited genealogist specializing in German research.

Fourthly, I became aware that there is an almost total public unawareness of the enormous number of double (and triple) German migrants who came to North America from Eastern Europe, whose descendants now number well over a million.

Many "German-Americans" identify with Germany as their ancestral homeland, even though there was no Germany, in the political sense, when their immigrant ancestors arrived and large numbers of emigrants arrived from areas which were never a part of Germany, before or after that period, most of them from the Russian Empire, but several hundred thousand also from the Austro-Hungarian Empire (mostly from outside Austria proper, as it exists today).

Even the Ellis Island Centennial Commission, whose members and staffers are presumably experts on immigration, has no provisions for properly honoring immigrants with a dual identity.

But more particularly, as a result of the extensive research I did as a co-author of the German Interest Group's *Research Guide to German-American Genealogy* (which covers Germans in practically every European country), I realized that there was no comprehensive English-language book on the market providing an overview of this distinctive group, even though there are some scholarly articles on specialized topics and the publications of organizations like the American Historical Society from Russia, the Germans from Russia Heritage Society and more recently established groups and publications, such as the Bukovina Society of the Americas, the East European Branch of the Manitoba Genealogical Society and *Wandering Volhynians: A Magazine for the Descendants of Germans from Volhynia and Poland*, have multiplied the amount of published material on this subject available in English.

I should add that Adam Giesinger has written an authoritative and comprehensive book, *From Catherine to Khrushchev: The Story of Russia's Germans*. G. C. Paikert's *The Danube Swabians: German Populations in Hungary, Rumania and Yugoslavia and Hitler's Impact on Their Patterns* (The Hague: Martinus Nijhoff, 1967) is excellent with respect to the history of these settlements. There are several books which deal with German settlements in particular areas of Romania in a genealogically valuable manner. For the area which used to be part of Hungary, the most detailed and comprehensive one is

Jacob Steigerwald's *Tracing Romania's Heterogeneous German Minority from Its Origins to the Diaspora* (Winona, MN: privately published, 1985). Heinz Lehmann's book, *The German Canadians, 1750-1937* (translated by Gerhard Bassler and published in English by Jesperson Press, St. John's, Newfoundland, in 1986) has a very helpful section on Austria-Hungary and Romania, but it is only 10 pages long. Despite all of these books, there is still a shortage of English-language historical material on the German settlements in East Central and Southeastern Europe.

Guides written for the specific purpose of helping genealogical researchers are even less adequate, despite the *AGoFF-Wegweiser*, the *Research Guide to German-American Genealogy* and the *Encyclopedia of German-American Genealogical Research* by Clifford Neal Smith and Anna Piszczan-Czaja Smith, which is out of print and a hard-to-get reference book.

Finally, when I got what I thought was an affordable opportunity to tour Poland, where my ancestors lived two homelands ago (with Ukraine as an intermediate homeland), I jumped at the chance and decided to add three weeks of scholarly research, chiefly at German archives and libraries specializing in Eastern European affairs, to see what scholarship is available in German.

Ill health and other commitments have delayed my intention to write a broad survey of the Germans in the East, whose immigrant descendants represented a goodly majority of the German-speakers in North Dakota and the Canadian Prairie Provinces, and a sizeable minority in the other Great Plains states, including Eastern Colorado. Thus I am writing shorter articles and books as foundation stones for my ultimate goal.

I had used whatever limited free time was available on our Eastern European group tour (focusing on, but not limited to, Poland) to visit archives, libraries and antique bookshops, wherever possible.

I had great luck at the Hungarian National Archives, where Dr. Imre Reš provided me with a good briefing, even though I arrived unannounced. He also gave me a personal copy of the English-language *Guide to the Archives of Hungary*, which is now out of print.

I immediately thought about how this information could be made available to North American genealogists. My first reaction was to xerox the sections on the Hungarian national archives (often referred to in Europe as state archives and, especially during the Communist era, central archives) and the regional (generally meaning county) archives. I also added the scattered addresses of the archives as a cut-and-paste job.

But after I received permission from the Hungarian Ministry of Culture and Public Instruction to disseminate this information, my ideas as to what could usefully be added grew and grew, especially as a result of my discovery of Prof. Wilhelm Winkler's 1927 statistical book on Germans in all countries while I was browsing through Wilson Library at the University of Minnesota. This book is the end result of these ideas. (It is, however, by no means as comprehensive a work as could result from lengthy scholarly research, so there are obviously a lot more items which could be added to it.)

The one English-language Hungarian-American genealogical guide, Jared Suess's *Handy Guide to Hungarian Genealogical Research* (Logan, UT: Everton Publishers, 1980), is quite different from this book, so the two are essentially complementary. His book lists several Hungarian-language gazetteers which show the various localities in Hungary, both in its present boundaries and in its pre-1919 boundaries; word lists in Hungarian, German and Latin; the Gothic, Cyrillic and Latin alphabets, with variations occurring in different languages; material on the history and language of Hungary; Hungarian personal names; administrative subdivisions of Hungarian counties; and sample documents and LDS catalog entries. Suess's *Central European Genealogical Terminology* (Logan, UT: Everton Publishers, 1978) is a useful dictionary, with numerous maps.

Moreover, people of all ethnic groups, including Germans, who are researching ancestors from Slovakia and the Carpatho-Ukraine (Ruthenia), are advised to look at *A Handbook of Czechoslovak Genealogical Research* by Daniel M. Schlyter. Duncan Gardiner's *German Towns in Slovakia & Upper Hungary* (Lakewood, OH: The Family Historian, 3rd ed., 1991) is the most valuable book on the history and location of German settlements in that area, with detailed maps, as well as useful historical and geographic information.

I am not aware of any genealogical guides or gazetteers for Romania, Serbia-Vojvodina, Croatia or Slovenia which are comparable to these books, although the *AGoFF-Wegweiser*, published in Germany, with the second edition translated into English, provides a great many addresses, maps and bibliographic entries. However, a number of very useful books dealing with the origins of German settlements are listed in Appendix 2.

Sources and Acknowledgments:

This project would, of course, never have gotten off the ground, were it not for the assistance and cooperation of the Hungarian National Archives and the permission given by the Hungarian Ministry of Culture and Public Instruction for me to reproduce the material which constituted Part I A of the first edition of this book and is the chief basis for the material in Parts I A and B in this second edition. For that, I express my grateful appreciation.

Part II consists of an updated list of addresses of archives provided by the responsible Hungarian Ministry. I should mention that I also included the branches of the various county archives, which were printed in the 1976 *Guide*, but were not on the list I received from Budapest in early 1992. They are thus correct as of 1976, but not necessarily in 1992. A description of selected materials in each archive has been added in the second edition, as explained in the preface.

The information I received from Budapest included material written in Hungarian, German and French. I had no problem with the German.

However, I would like to thank my son, Bruce Brandt, for assistance in translating the French material and in typing the list of addresses, which required the creation of Hungarian diacritical marks which were not on the fonts we had for our word processor.

I would also like to express my appreciation to Paul Rupprecht, whose knowledge of Hungarian came to my attention through the newsletter of the Friends of the Immigration History Research Center, to which we both belong. The center, which focuses on immigrants from Eastern and Southern Europe, is located in St. Paul and affiliated with the University of Minnesota. Mr. Rupprecht proofread the addresses of the archives and corrected both spelling and translations. He also provided me with books which were helpful in preparing the maps and the dateline of historical events.

Since the Hungarian *Guide* dealt with the contents of the archives as a whole, without any particular focus on genealogically relevant material, I added, as Part I C in this edition, a summary of key information included in the LDS (Church of Jesus Christ of Latter-day Saints) 1979 Research Paper on "Records of Genealogical Value for Hungary." Part I D represents specific genealogical information which I received from the Hungarian National Archives in January 1991, most of which was included in the *Research Guide to German-American Genealogy*.

Parts I and II of the book are equally relevant for all genealogists, regardless of ethnicity, interested in obtaining information from Hungarian archives. In fact, most of this material is useful for all archival researchers, regardless of what they are researching. This is even more true of the second than of the first edition.

Since my particular interest, however, concerned the Germans in Hungary, I added the information at the end (appendices, tables and maps) specifically for those who are researching German ancestors or German settlements more generally.

The dateline of historical events was drawn from many sources, but I relied most heavily on the books by G. C. Paikert and Jacob Steigerwald. Suess's handbook on Hungary has a quite different dateline of historic events, with more emphasis on political and military history, but less emphasis on the German settlements in Hungary. The statistical tables are based very largely on Prof. Wilhelm Winkler's substantial tome. The maps were adapted from those in books I borrowed from Paul Rupprecht, with another map which I received from Martha Remer Connor added in the second edition.

Duplication:

Part I A of the first edition was reprinted by permission of the Hungarian Ministry of Culture and Public Instruction. The second edition contains only a short portion of the text of the *Guide to the Archives of Hungary*, but this book remains the basis for most of the material in Parts I and II of this edition. Authorization should be sought from the Hungarian Ministry for any further reproduction of material from its *Guide*. The rest of the book may not be reproduced without permission from the publisher, although anyone is, of course, free to consult the original sources for such use as may be desired. However, since the sharing of information is the essence of genealogy, permission to make copies of limited amounts of material for educational, rather than commercial, purposes is hereby granted. I want to help, not hinder, other authors, speakers and researchers in the community of genealogists.

Coverage of Hungary Before and After World War I:

Much of the material in this book deals only with contemporary Hungary, but other parts deal with historic Hungary (i.e., Greater Hungary within its pre-Trianon borders).

While the various Hungarian archives obviously have more information about persons and events in what is now Hungary, at least some of the archives also include information on territories ceded to other countries after World War I. If it is these other areas you are researching, I would advise you to contact the Hungarian National Archives as a first step.

Notes on Ethnicity and Inter-Ethnic Relations:

The Germans were by no means the only ethnic group which settled in areas where they were a minority. For example, there are also large numbers of Magyars (the term for ethnic Hungarians, as contrasted with citizens of Hungary) in Southern Slovakia, Northern and Western Romania, the Vojvodina and Eastern Croatia.

In fact, nearly every ethnic group had such settlers in foreign-speaking territory, although some had only a few and some a great many.

These national minorities were of two kinds:

(1) those along border areas, where there was sometimes a rather checkered pattern of local majorities vs. minorities

(2) those who settled in ethnic islands far from their linguistic homeland

The first kind of minority was common in Europe, especially Eastern Europe, and made the application of President Wilson's principle of national self-determination far more complex in practice than in theory. Since other parts of Wilson's Fourteen Points at times conflicted with the idea of self-determination and since the goals of the European Allies were by no means always Wilsonian, this created additional problems.

However, as far as the "islanders" were concerned ("colonists" was a term used widely and officially to describe foreign-language, especially German, settlers), the Germans differed from other nationalities in that:

(1) They had a vastly larger number of such emigrants than any other European ethnic group (except, of course, for the unique status of the Jews, who were minorities, but numbering in the millions in Eastern Europe, wherever they went).

(2) These "islands" were often hundreds, even thousands, of miles from any territory where German was spoken by the majority, so these "colonists" maintained the German language and customs as of the date of emigration and to the extent that these changed (as they inevitably did, though often to a surprisingly small degree), the changes were quite different from the way the German language and customs developed in the Germanic core of Central Europe.

I might also add a postscript concerning the somewhat ambiguous connection between "Germans" and "Jews." The Yiddish language spoken by the Jews was a derivative of Old High German. Many Jews went to Eastern Europe from Germany or Austria (though sometimes this was an intermediate stop for Jews from farther west) and later many returned to Germany and especially Austria from the East. Members of the two groups were often the co-developers of East European cities and industries, either simultaneously or sequentially. At various times and in various places (especially those under German or

Austrian rule, even where the Germans were a minority), the Jews also used the German language.

For many non-mainstream religious groups, which included dissident Christians like my Mennonite ancestors as well as Jews, religion, not nationality or ethnicity, was the key factor in the group's own self-identification (as well as how others identified it).

The relevance of this for ethnic statistics is that in some censuses or statistical reports, the Jews in Eastern Europe were counted as Germans; in others they were not.

In view of the fact that the Jews had been forced to take up trades in the towns during the Middle Ages, when they were forbidden to own land, and this tradition continued in most areas, the inclusion or exclusion of Jews as Germans would have made very little difference in rural Hungary, where the vast majority of people lived until the second half of the eighteenth century, because there were virtually no Jewish farmers and only a few Jews in the small or medium-sized towns.

Only in Budapest (as far as Hungary is concerned) would this have been a major factor in determining the number of "Germans." In fact, in 1906 some 23% of the people of Budapest were Jews by religion, while only 9.3% were Germans by ethnicity, so the vast majority of Jews obviously were not identified as ethnic Germans. But in 1848, when Budapest had a predominantly German population, the situation could have been quite different.

I should also note that what applied to Greater Hungary in this respect did not apply to the areas to the northeast of Hungary, ruled by Austria or Russia, where there were far more Jews in relatively small towns.

Two Hungarian-American genealogical societies, serving members of all ethnic groups whose ancestors came from Hungary, have been formed since the publication of the first edition of this book.

They are:

>Hungarian Genealogical Society of America
>Kathy Karocki, President
>124 Esther St.
>Toledo, OH 43605-1435
>(publishes *Hungarian Genealogical Society of America Newsletter*)

Hungarian/American Friendship Society
Douglas P. Holmes, President
2811 Elvyra Way # 236
Sacramento, CA 95821-5865
(publishes *Régi Magyarország*, meaning "Old Hungary")

Both societies are members of the Federation of East European Family History Societies, P.O. Box 21346, Salt Lake City, UT 84121-0346, which I helped found. This federation has, among its goals, (1) facilitating the dissemination of information about the rapid changes in the ex-Communist countries with respect to the availability of genealogical resources and researchers, and (2) promoting harmony within and among the various ethnic and religious groups, particularly genealogical societies devoted to researching ancestors from Eastern Europe.

FEEFHS has published a newsletter since December 1992. It has also published a *Resource Guide to East European Genealogy*, which will be updated twice a year and is available from John D. Movius, P.O. Box 4327, Davis, CA 95617-4327. The guide provides a brief description of the rapidly growing number of organizations (currently more than 60 from 7 countries) and data on professional genealogists and translators specializing in Eastern Europe.

Assimilation vs. Maintenance of a Separate Identity by Minorities:

Those who moved to foreign lands during the Middle Ages usually became assimilated over time. Among Germans, there were two major exceptions: (1) the Transylvanian Saxons and (2) the Baltic Germans.

The first group consisted of free men, who owned their own land and never experienced the feudal servitude which was almost universal in Europe, so they obviously had a great stake in the maintenance of their status.

The second group came as a ruling group, and remained an elite even after these countries came under the domination of other rulers, particularly the Russian Czars, whom they served in top-level military and civilian positions in disproportionate numbers.

For the most part, the Germans who moved eastward after the Reformation retained their own identity. This was slightly less true of Catholics, who were often co-religionists of the ethnic majority.

However, this was never much of an issue between the Germans and the host majority until the French Revolution unloosed the explosive forces of nationalism. In fact, prior to that, the

Germans were usually welcomed as people who brought more advanced techniques from the West.

This began to change in 1789, although at first only among the elites. The average person (at least outside France), and especially in Eastern Europe, did not develop a strong sense of nationalism until later. (This does not mean that rulers were unaware of the potential significance of ethnic factors before 1789.)

However, the Revolutions of 1830 certainly had a nationalistic feature in some cities and those of 1848 were often highly nationalistic, although their principal goal was freedom. But for the most part, these revolutionary elements came from the middle class and intellectual circles. They were not really uprisings of the common people.

Still, it was the attitudes of the authorities which counted for much more than the attitudes of the people, in terms of how minorities were treated, at least until the last third of the nineteenth century.

Basically, there were two approaches to the assimilation of national minorities:

(1) Hungary, like Prussia and later Russia, sought to force assimilation, in good measure by control over education. (There was forced assimilation of religious minorities in Spain and other countries before 1789, but rarely did this affect ethnic groups as such.)

(2) The Austrian government, on the other hand, was determinedly anti-assimilationist in its policies, because Germans constituted only a minority in the polyglot empire; thus attempts to force assimilation were likely to cause resentment and, therefore, a threat to the unity of the empire. This pattern was similar, though for different reasons, to the predominant policies of the pre-nationalist era, perhaps exemplified best by Poland-Lithuania.

We might compare these with the two somewhat different assimilationist developments in North America.

(1) The American "melting pot" was largely a matter of voluntary choice by the immigrants, because they perceived this as the route to betterment. Not until 1917, when the United States entered World War I, did government policies force assimilation, particularly for Germans, when many states forbade the teaching of German in a wave of anti-German hysteria.

(2) Canada, on the other hand, prides itself in being a "mosaic," where, for example, cohesive French, German and Ukrainian communities exist peacefully next to each other.

In reality, of course, the American "melting pot" never did away with ethnic communities to the extent theorized. On the other hand, considerably more assimilation has taken place in Canada than the "mosaic" implies. Nevertheless, the difference between the two countries is real, even if the models are not pure reality.

This very problem of assimilation vs. continued ethnic distinctiveness, with equal rights, lies at the heart of most of the conflicts in Eastern Europe (and in the rest of the world, for that matter) today. History leaves no doubt in my mind as to which kind of government policy is most conducive to peace and harmony.

German by Speech vs. German by Origin:

The data in the Winkler book come from censuses which show how many people spoke German at home as their mother tongue. (Many other statistical records use a similar definition of ethnicity.)

The pressure for Magyarization in Hungary and the opportunities for government positions offered by assimilation undoubtedly led a significant number of former German-speakers to adopt Hungarian as their mother tongue, although this would be most true of Budapest and less true of medium-sized cities and towns, while it would hardly have applied to the rural areas at all, at least until the twentieth century. (This policy was, however, clearly one of the reasons why a significantly higher percentage of members of minority groups than of ethnic Magyars emigrated from Hungary to North America.)

Because of this policy, the number of people of German origin is certainly understated by the definition of ethnicity used for the census.

Interestingly enough, we have our own unique version of such discrepancies in North America. For example, North Dakota is not a very German state if the definition of a German is someone whose ancestors immigrated from Germany, even if we mean the territory of the former German Empire by that. On the other hand, it is one of our most German states if we used early twentieth-century data on the language spoken at home as the criterion.

The explanation is that the vast majority of German-speaking immigrants to North Dakota came from Eastern Europe, especially the Russian Empire, but also Hungary.

Village Lineage Books (Ortssippenbücher):

Interest in genealogy has grown in Germany, just as it has in North America. The Germans who left Eastern Europe voluntarily or involuntarily have certainly been a leading force in this movement, because the history and genealogy of their hometowns in the East would have been lost rather quickly if they did not assemble what information they could. At least, this was true during the Communist era. The continuing uncertainty as to how many parish registers were destroyed and the rapid assimilation of the Easterners into the German mainstream will continue to be a motivating factor in this regard, even though the doors to the archives in Eastern Europe are now readily accessible in most cases.

There is a 1991 edition of a book by Franz Heinzmann, *Die Ortssippenbücher in Deutschland* (published by the Franz Heinzmann Verlag in Düsseldorf) which lists the village lineage books which have been published. Unfortunately, I don't know how much coverage of German settlements in the East is included in this book. However, quite a few such books for former German villages in Eastern Europe have been published or are available in manuscript form.

Recommendations for Future Editions or Publications:

The Hungarian Ministry of Culture and Public Instruction indicated that a new edition of the *Guide to the Archives of Hungary* was planned and it welcomed my recommendations for making the book more helpful to American users.

I likewise welcome any recommendations (as well as corrections) for this book, which I plan to make available until the new edition of the Hungarian *Guide* appears. I might add that I have not gone to great effort to ensure consistency in place names, which may be listed in German, Hungarian, or any other language if currently applicable, or two or more of these, although I have attempted to give both the Hungarian and the German names of key localities in the text. But hopefully Appendix 1 will clarify any possible confusion on this point.

                                        Edward Reimer Brandt

Minneapolis, Minnesota
Revised May 1993

PART I

OVERVIEW OF GENEALOGICAL RECORDS AVAILABLE IN HUNGARIAN ARCHIVES

A. Key Dates in Hungarian History for Purposes of Archival Research

B. General Description of the Contents of the Regional Archives, with Pertinent Historical and Governmental Background Information

C. Description of the Contents and Organization of the Hungarian National Archives

D. Archival Records of Particular Genealogical Value, According to the LDS Family History Library

E. Current Information Regarding Genealogical Research in or on Hungary

A. KEY DATES IN HUNGARIAN HISTORY FOR PURPOSES OF ARCHIVAL RESEARCH

A dateline of historic events can be found in Appendix 2. However, there are a few crucial dividing lines in Hungarian history which you must bear in mind in reviewing descriptions of archival material, viz.:

1526 The Turks defeated the Hungarians at the Battle of Mohács and took over most of Hungary, which dated back to 896.
1699 The Treaty of Karlowitz returned control of most of Hungary to the Hapsburg emperors, who had also become kings of Hungary in 1526.
1848 The revolutions which swept through most of Europe also included Hungary. Their main goal was freedom and they ended feudalism in the Austro-Hungarian Empire. While they had a nationalistic element, the conflict was by no means strictly along ethnic lines.
1867 The Compromise of 1867 created the Austro-Hungarian (Dual) Monarchy, whereby Hungary obtained self-government in domestic affairs, although the Hapsburg emperor continued to be the Hungarian monarch.
1920 The Treaty of Trianon, following World War I, transferred a major portion of Hungarian territory to Czechoslovakia, Romania, Yugoslavia and Austria.
1947 A Communist government was installed in Hungary after World War II.
1989 Communism collapsed in Hungary.

To be sure, listing a single date for some of these events is an oversimplification. For example, the conquest of Hungary by the Turks and its reconquest from the Turks did not occur in a single year, with somewhat different dates applying to different parts of the country. Some other events also included transitional phases which lasted more than a year.

Nevertheless, these are key dates to remember and the events will be referred to repeatedly.

B. GENERAL DESCRIPTION OF THE CONTENTS OF REGIONAL ARCHIVES, WITH PERTINENT HISTORICAL AND GOVERNMENTAL BACKGROUND INFORMATION

Hungary has been divided into counties for 1,000 years. In the feudal period there were first royal counties, then nobilitary ones (under the authority of the king and the nobles, respectively).

After 1848 there were county municipalities, but the major cities (called royal free cities originally, later municipal cities) were independent of the counties.

Today only Budapest has an independent status and archives, while the other cities and their archives are subordinate to the county. However, there are still references to city archives as separate divisions within the county archives.

Moreover, one must distinguish between the unified administration of archives and their physical location, since archives under the same jurisdiction may be at two or more different places.

For genealogists, the most significant aspect of county or regional archives (the terms are used interchangeably, except for the inclusion of Budapest in the latter) are that these archives have duplicates of the parish registers from 1828 to 1895 and copies of the state's civil registers since then.

The county and Budapest archives are also entitled to take over the archival material of administrative, judicial, prosecutorial and economic organs, institutes, institutions and associations formerly active in the county or city. Moreover, they have gathered many personal or family papers.

It is important to recognize that almost all of the counties have undergone boundary changes in the twentieth century and many of them have had their names changed, sometimes more than once, chiefly as a result of consolidation and, less often, separation.

The most substantial reorganization occurred after the 1920 Treaty of Trianon and the subsequent plebiscite in the Burgenland, which resulted in Hungary ceding territory to Czechoslovakia (now Slovakia); Romania (including Transylvania); Yugoslavia (originally known as the Kingdom of Serbs, Croats and Slovenes), specifically the Vojvodina, an autonomous province of Serbia, as well as most of Croatia and a small corner of Northeastern Slovenia, both now independent nations; and Austria. Bosnia-Herzegovina, which had been administered by the imperial (joint Austro-Hungarian) government also became part of Yugoslavia.

Frequently the application of the principle of national self-determination split counties between Hungary and other countries after World War I.

In earlier times, religious chapters and convents generally had the legal right and responsibility for authenticating documents and records. Regional authorities are now in charge of this.

Prior to the fall of Communism, the archives were divided into periods separated by the Revolution of 1848, which resulted in the total and permanent abolition of feudalism, and the takeover of Communism after World War II. The 1976 *Guide* refers to the three periods as feudal, capitalistic or bourgeois, and socialist, respectively.

Of course, the establishment of the Austro-Hungarian (Dual) Monarchy in 1867, after which Hungary had a government which was independent from that of Austria in most respects, also produced some changes.

In going back to the "feudal" period, one must recognize 1526, when the Turks defeated Hungary at the Battle of Mohács (where the Hungarian king was killed, leading to Hapsburg rule of Hungary), as perhaps the most significant dividing point in Hungarian history, with strong implications for archival records. During the 15 years after that, the Turks conquered most of Hungary, with the Hapsburgs retaining control over a small sliver in Western and Northern Hungary, but only by paying a tribute to the Ottoman Turkish emperor. Since the Turks besieged Vienna twice, even the "free" parts of Hungary (or most of them) were temporarily under Turkish occupation.

The tide turned in 1683, when the second siege of Vienna was repulsed, and by 1718 the Hapsburgs had gained control of nearly all of the historic territory of Hungary, even though border skirmishes continued for several decades. Thus the 150 to 200 years of Turkish rule probably left an even greater impact on Hungary than the drastic truncation of Hungary by the Treaty of Trianon in 1920. You will find many references to pre- and post-Mohács Hungary, as well as to pre- and post-Trianon Hungary.

County municipalities and municipal cities are classified in the same series of archival groups because of their earlier equal legal status.

The pre-1848 material of the regional archives generally includes the following (except for destruction due to war or other causes): records of the Lord Lieutenant (administrator, royal commissioner), the nobilitary assembly and its various committees (dealing with economic matters, orphans, insurrections, etc.), the administration of Emperor Joseph II (1780-90), the first and second sub-prefect, the tax collector, the comptroller, the orphans' court, the chief medical officer, the engineer, the judicial tribunal, and the chief public attorney.

During the 1848-49 Revolution, a temporary committee or county commission replaced the nobilitary assembly, but the various functionally specialized offices continued to function as before. Commissioners of the revolutionary government left records of great value.

From 1850 to 1860 the Imperial-Royal County Authorities and chief constables served as administrators and the Imperial-Royal Tribunals and District Courts as adjudicators.

After the transitional period associated with the Compromise of 1867 (whereby Hungary obtained self-government in domestic affairs), a new form of administration was introduced in 1872. A substantial amount of material was produced and preserved during the 1872-1944 period. In addition to the special offices which existed before 1848, the autonomous municipal commission, the finance office, the auditing office, the veterinary surgeon, the social [should it be school?] inspector, the administrative committee, and the chief district constables are listed as generating material preserved by the county archives.

The county archives also include collections of county and village by-laws, the rules governing associations, the work plans regarding forests, the records of water conservation, and the registers of public roads.

The pre-1848 material of independent municipal cities (mostly free royal cities at the time, i.e., subject only to the king, who was the Hapsburg emperor) include records of the elected commission, the inner (executive) council, the various specialized commissions (economic affairs, orphans, fire protection, allocation of soldiers, etc.), those of special offices (tax office, chamberlain, orphans' court, audit, customs, engineering), and of the city court. Secret archives also existed. The special city offices continued to function from 1849 to 1871, but under different authorities: the community council (1850-60), the commission again (1860-61), the elected burgesses (1862-67) and by the assembly of the city authority, with the council continuing to work during this period.

After 1872 the cities, like the counties, had a Lord Lieutenant, a municipal commission, and several functionally specialized commissions.

The records of *towns and villages*, subordinate to the county administration, are now in the custody of the county archives. Though they have serious gaps and deficiencies, they are nevertheless indispensable sources of local history.

The archival material of the feudal boroughs includes journals and acts of the council, the accounts and records of the chief magistrate, the records of the public tutor, the city chamberlain, the tax collector, and the police commissioner. There is very little pre-1848 village material (judge's accounts, tax assessments, a publication book, etc.).

There is more material for the post-1848 period, mostly journals and acts of the body of representatives (relatively complete) and the records of the council and the mayor's office, but relatively little from the special offices. Records of village administration and taxation are fragmentary.

From the 1870s to 1950 the administration of specialized functions at the county and sub-county levels was under the jurisdiction of numerous *special state offices*, independent of the local government (e.g., county and district fire inspectors were subject to the Ministry of the Interior. This system was highly complex, but very centralized.

Of particular interest may be the fact that schools were under the supervision of the District Inspectorate of Schools (which supervised public schools in several counties), the County Inspectorate of Schools (for elementary schools) and regional school inspectorates.

Archival groups of *jurisdiction* include records of courts (tables, tribunals and district courts), two levels of prosecuting offices, penal and correctional institutes, and public notaries.

The most valuable material in the archival groups of *institutes and institutions* pertains to a great variety of elementary, special education, secondary and vocational schools, as well as general and specialized post-secondary institutions. You should be aware that terms like "high school" (a post-secondary institution, meaning "higher education") and "public school" (which does not necessarily mean a school operated and financed by the state) do not always have the same meaning in Europe as in North America. The Hungarian school system includes schools designated by terms similar to those in other continental European countries, e.g., "lyceum" and "Realschule."

There is only a small amount of material from cultural, as distinct from educational, institutions.

The series of archival groups of *corporations* consists mostly of feudal guild papers and later records of professional, business, agricultural and forestry organizations, as well as social welfare institutions.

Only fragments of the papers of *associations* (which appear to be distinguished from corporations and cultural institutions by a fine line, since they seem to overlap) have been preserved.

The small series of archival groups of *economic organs* deals partly with post-1945 state enterprises. The older records are those of individual industrial, commercial and economic enterprises, including large farms, as distinct from collective groups.

The archival groups of *ecclesiastical organs* are significant especially because of the church's former role in authenticating documents and events. Most such archives have records of extinct male and female convents.

Family archives have come into the hands of regional archives through salvage from the events of war, deposit, gift or purchase. Records of major land-owning families are in the national archives.

The papers of private individuals constitute the small *personal archival groups*.

All regional archives also preserve *collections*, with a special emphasis on pre-1526 charters, with finding aids to facilitate research. There are separate collections of manuscript maps and, in some archives, photographs and press collections.

The few preserved records of the 1919 (Communist) *Hungarian Councils' Republic* are in distinct archival groups.

The post-World War II records may be of interest to historians and social scientists, but they are irrelevant to genealogical research, with rare exceptions.

There are published finding aids for (1) the lists of archival groups, (2) manuscript maps, and (3) feudal conscriptions (tax assessments) to be found in the regional archives.

C. DESCRIPTION OF THE CONTENTS AND ORGANIZATION OF THE HUNGARIAN NATIONAL ARCHIVES

The pre-1526 Hungarian Royal Archives were annihilated during the Turkish conquest (1541-1686). Although the Vienna archives of the Hapsburg dynasty, which ruled Hungary after 1526, contain some pertinent material (especially with respect to German, and smaller numbers of other non-Magyar, settlers in the largely depopulated territory reconquered from the Turks), most of the records for 1526-1756 were kept by the Counts Palatine, but these were not numerous.

The "ancient" national archives (described as records of the 1756-1874 period) were transferred from Pozsony (Bratislava, Slovakia) to Buda in 1785. After 1867 these were absorbed into what became known as the Hungarian Royal National Archives, with the word "Royal" dropped in 1946, when a republic was established. In 1957 the archives came under the supervision of the Ministry of Culture (which means Education and Culture in various continental European countries).

The library of the National Archives is divided into the following *sections and groups* (or sub-sections):

(1) Section I preserves the records of the central organs of government from 1526 to 1867.
(2) Section II contains such records for 1867-1944.
(3) Section III keeps the records of families, corporations and non-governmental bodies prior to 1945. In addition, it has several special collections, e.g., records from before 1526 and maps.
(4) Section IV has the records of economic enterprises, primarily pre-Communist private businesses.
(5) Section V includes three groups. Of primary interest to the researcher is the one which keeps the microfilm collection (which includes records from national, local and foreign sources) and has the xeroxing facilities. The Cabinet for source studies is responsible for publications. It prepares monographs and studies of historical sources. The Record Cadaster Section surveys pre-1526 archival material preserved in Hungary and abroad, and produces finding aids.

At the end of 1974 the archives had over 30,000 running meters of material, with half in Section I, one-fourth in Section II, and the rest divided almost evenly between Sections III and IV. The number of negative microfilm exposures was almost 28,000.

The material in the archives is divided into structural units (lettered *sections* to distinguish them from the foregoing), *archives, archival groups and archival subgroups*, in descending order of size.

The structural units are responsible for the following lettered sections, as described below:

```
Section I      for Sections A-I and N-O
Section II     for Sections K-L
Section III    for Sections P-V
Section IV     for Section Z
Section V      for Section X
Bureau         for Section Y
```

The contents of the sections are described the *Guide* exactly as listed below (except for bracketed material, which indicates summarized or inserted material). Please note that "J" and "W" are not listed and that the descriptions are not all in alphabetical order.

> Section "A" is the archives of the Hungarian Chancellery. It contains the records of the organ of government of Hungary at the Viennese court, the Royal Hungarian Court Chancellery, together with those of offices and persons organically connected with it from 1527 to 1848.
>
> Section "B" is the archives of the Transylvanian Chancellery. It contains the records of the organ of government of Transylvania at the Viennese court, the Royal Transylvanian Court Chancellery, together with those of offices and persons organically connected with it from 1686 to 1848.
>
> Section "C" is the archives of the Locotenential Council. It contains the records of the national administrative authority of Hungary, the Royal Hungarian Locotenential Council, together with those of offices and persons organically connected with it from 1724 to 1848.
>
> Section "D" is the archives of the age of absolutism. It keeps the records partly of Austrian ministries in Vienna, but mainly of courtly, national and regional governmental bodies in Hungary, some military, but the majority civil, from the period of the so-called neo-absolutism between 1848 and 1867. Here are the archival groups of the Royal Hungarian and the Royal Transylvanian Court Chancelleries, restored in 1860 and of the Royal Hungarian Locotenential Council, reconstituted in 1861. However, the records of the financial organization of Hungary are not here but in the section "E", and the archival groups of the central bodies of Transylvanian government are attached to section "F", even if they are derived from the period of neo-absolutism.
>
> Section "E" is called: Archives of the Hungarian treasuries. It comprises several archives and some archival groups belonging to no archives.

The archives of the Hungarian Chamber contains the records of the most important national financial body, the Royal Hungarian Chamber (from 1748 Court Chamber), united with the Locotenential Council between 1785 and 1790, also those of offices organically connected with it from 1529 to 1848.

In the archives of the Hungarian Chamber one finds archival groups of mixed provenance, having the character of collections, among them the records of the Hungarian Chamber itself, further of ecclesiastical bodies, families and persons, even from the time after 1848 when the Chamber did not exist. This archives contains the collections most frequently used by students of the feudal period after 1526 (*Urbaria et conscriptiones, Conscriptiones portarum, Regesta decimarum, Neoregistrata acta*, etc.).

The archives of the Szepes Chamber embraces the records of the second national financial body of feudal Hungary and of the offices organically connected with it from 1551 to 1813. This Chamber acted as a cameral directorate (so-called administration) in certain periods.

Outside the framework of archives section "E" contains also the papers of other cameral administrations and of some cameral offices of a minor level.

In the financial archives of the age of absolutism one finds the records of the central and regional bodies of finance administration in Hungary and partly in the Serbian Voivodate [Vojvodina] between 1848 and 1867.

The fourth archives comprised in section "E" is the archives of the royal directorate of legal affairs. Here are the records of the body safeguarding the rights and interests of the treasury and also of the state, the royal directorate of legal affairs, together with those of regional and local offices and persons organically connected with it and with its successors, mainly from the last third of the eighteenth and the first two thirds of the nineteenth century.

Section "F" embraces the archives of the national governmental organs of Transylvania. Two of these archives belonged to authenticating authorities (*loca credibilia*): one is the national archives of the Gyulafehérvár chapter, the other is that of Kolozsmonostor convent. Both contain records up to 1868, among them fragments of the archives of the national Princes of Transylvania. The bulk of the section consists of the archives containing records of the national central governmental organs of the Transylvanian Principate [Principality] (under Hapsburg rule from 1690) and of offices and persons organically connected with them. These are: the archives of the *Guvernium Transylvanicum*, of the General Commissariat of Transylvania, of the General

Audit Office of Transylvania and of the Transylvanian Treasury.

The records of the national, regional and local authorities of Transylvania, active in 1848 and during the neo-absolutism between 1849 and 1867, among them those of the *Gubernium* restored in 1861, are preserved in separate archives.

This section, extending earlier than 1526 and somewhat later than 1867, embraces a few archival groups outside the archives too.

Section "G" unites the archives of two fights for freedom: those led by Imre THÖKÖLY [1671] and Ferenc RÁKÓCZI II [1703-11]. It contains the material of their organizations of government together with their personal and family papers from the middle of the seventeenth century to 1712 inclusively.

Section "H" is the archives of the 1848/49 "Ministry". It preserves the records of the first ministerial government in Hungary and of offices and persons organically connected with it, also of other authorities and offices active during the fight for freedom. Some papers of a few counties and cities from 1848/49 are also kept here.

Section "I" is called: Records transferred from the Vienna archives. This section holds records delivered from the central Austrian archives to Hungary according to an agreement made with Austria after the dissolution of the Monarchy, and not allotted to other sections. Their most important part comes from the archives of the ruler's cabinet.

Section "N" is called *Archiwum regnicolare*, i.e. the material of the "ancient" national archives before the 1874 reorganization. It contains three archives: those of the Count Palatine, the Chief Justice and "the country".

The Palatine's archives embrace the papers of the Counts Palatine from 1554 to 1848. Those of the Archduke Joseph have the largest size, comprising also the 1828 national conscription.

The papers of the Chief Justices cover the years 1586 to 1849.

In the archives of "the country" the most valuable parts are the records of the diets and of parliamentary commissions, those of the regulations of frontiers and the national conscriptions of 1715 and 1720.

Section "N" contains also two archival groups after 1874.

Section "O" is called: Judicial archives. This section contains the archives of the royal, i.e. central courts of law of feudal Hungary after 1526: those of the *Curia*, the *Personalis*, the protonotary of the count palatine, the protonotary of the Chief Justice, the *Magister tavernicorum*. Here is the remaining fragment of the archives of the Transylvanian Royal Table; also the archives of the four district tables of Hungary. This section preserves not only the records of the central courts of Hungary from the era of neo-absolutism, but also those of the Vienna Ministry of Justice and the Supreme Court, pertaining to Hungary and Transylvania, also those of several regional courts and attorneys.

Section "K" is called: Archives of central governmental bodies of the bourgeois period. Here the records of the central governmental bodies of Hungary from 1867 to 1944 together with those of offices and persons organically connected with them are kept in the following archives:

Archives of the Parliament,
Archives of the offices of the King (Regent),
Archives of the Prime Minister's office,
Archives of the Ministry of Foreign Affairs,
Archives of the Ministry of the Interior,
Archives of the Ministry of Agriculture, Industry and Commerce,
Archives of the Ministry of Public Works and Transport,
Archives of the Ministry of Agriculture,
Archives of the Ministry of Commerce,
Archives of the Ministry of Industry,
Archives of the Ministry of Food,
Archives of the Ministry of Finance,
Archives of the Ministry of Religious Affairs and Education,
Archives of the Ministry of Justice,
Press Archives.

All the three branches of government: legislation, administration and jurisdiction are represented among the bodies which have produced the archival groups of the enumerated archives. The section has also a few archival groups outside of archives.

Section "L" contains the archives of two people's commissariats of the 1919 Republic of Councils: that of Agriculture and that of Finance. The records of the remaining people's commissariats are found in the material of the respective Ministries.

The Archives has no section with the sign "M". Prior to 1970 there was one, containing records after 1944, the material of the Section of the People's Democracy. In 1970 this Section was transformed to the New Hungarian Central Archives.

Section "P" is called: Archives of families, corporations and institutions. This section contains the following major family archives:

Archives of the Balassa family
Archives of the Batthyány family
Archives of the Esterházy family
Archives of the Festetics family
Archives of the Habsburg family
Archives of the Károlyi family
Archives of the Széchenyi family
Archives of the Teleki family
Archives of the Zichy family

One finds in this section the papers of freemasonic organizations, of some ecclesiastical corporations, of numerous associations, scientific and cultural institutions and of many persons.

Section "Q" is the collection Pre-Mohács, embracing the most valuable collection of the Archives, representing the most ancient material: the Diplomatic Archives. This collection contains records before 1526, selected from different sections of the National Archives, approaching 108,000 in number. The Diplomatic Archives is the most important source basis for pre-1526 Hungarian history.

The name of section "R" is: Post-1526 collection. The material of this section is related to that of section "P"; the majority is made up of archival groups of families and persons. Its most valuable part is the Kossuth Archives, containing the papers of Lajos Kossuth. Equally significant, but of a smaller size is the Klapka Archives, made up of the legacy of György Klapka, general in the 1848/49 freedom fight.

Section "S" is the collection of maps. It unites under one management maps selected from various parts of the Archives, both from the feudal and the bourgeois period.

Section "T" is the collection of plans. It has a character similar to the collection of maps, and includes plans and drawings.

Section "U" is the photographic collection. It contains exposures made of archival material at home and abroad.

Section "V" is the collection of seals. It embraces seals applied to archival material, imprints and squeeze moldings of such. Most of them are squeeze moldings made from the seals of the Archives prior to 1526.

Section "Z" is the Economic Archives. It contains mainly the archival groups of economic organizations of the bourgeois period. It was established in 1962 from the material of the then abolished Economic Archives, and has been enlarged since. The principal types of economic organizations producing its material are: [banks, savings banks, mortgage banks, credit unions, insurance companies, business associations, merchandise and stock exchanges, mining companies, iron and steel companies, and machine factories].

Section "X" is the film archives. Its holdings total almost 28 million exposures. [This includes material from public, church and foreign archives.]

Finally section "Y" contains the files of the Archives' own administration.

Numerous books and articles relating to the national archives and their contents have been published.

D. ARCHIVAL RECORDS OF PARTICULAR GENEALOGICAL VALUE, ACCORDING TO THE LDS FAMILY HISTORY LIBRARY

Since the *Guide to the Archives of Hungary* is a general description of archival holdings and does not concentrate on those of specific genealogical value, key information for the genealogical researcher is here extracted or summarized from the short research paper, "Records of Genealogical Value for Hungary," Series C, Research Paper No. 17, published in 1979 by the Genealogical Department of the Church of Jesus Christ of Latter-day Saints, Salt Lake City.

1. <u>Civil registration</u>
   Dates: since 1895
   Location: Local civil registrar, with duplicates in the county archives
   Key data: Birth and marriage records list names of parents; marriage records list date and place of birth; deaths list name of surviving spouse and parents; all records list date and place of event

2. <u>Poorhouse and hospital records</u>
   Dates: 1873-1920
   Location: County archives
   Key data: Names of patient and parents; age and residence of patient (some records not in useable order)

3. <u>Land records and deeds (Intabulations-Bücher)</u>
   Dates: ca. 1750-1945
   Location: 1750-1850 in national archives; 1850-1945 in county archives
   Key data: Names of landowners and successors

4. <u>Land registration records (tax assessments)</u>
   Dates: 1715-1945
   Location: 1715-1900 in national archives; 1900-45 in county archives and courthouses
   Key data: Name of property owner or head of family, sometimes names of family members

5. <u>Tax books</u>
   Dates: ca. 1700-now
   Location: 1715-1900 in national archives; since 1900 in county archives and courthouses
   Key data: Name and residence

6. <u>Parish registers</u>
   Dates: Catholic since 1700; Lutherans, Reformed and Greek Orthodox since early 1700s
   Location: Local parishes; on film at Family History Library, Salt Lake City
   Key data: Birth and christening records list date and place of birth, name and residence of parents (sometimes also parental age, place of birth and religion)

7. **Synagogue registers**
   Dates: since ca. 1850
   Location: Local synagogues; on film at Salt Lake City
   Key data: Same as for parish registers, except no christenings

8. **Wills**
   Dates: 1600-1900
   Location: National archives
   Key data: Names of testators and heirs

9. **Nobility records**
   Dates: early 1400s-1900
   Location: National and county archives
   Key data: Name, title, residence and position

E. CURRENT INFORMATION REGARDING GENEALOGICAL RESEARCH IN OR ON HUNGARY

Since both the *Guide to the Archives of Hungary* and the LDS paper on "Records of Genealogical Value for Hungary" were published in the 1970s, more recent information gathered for the *Research Guide to German-American Genealogy*, published by the German Interest Group (now the Germanic Genealogy Society) in 1991, as supplemented by information I obtained during my 1991 East European trip and by the 1994 *Resource Guide to East European Genealogy*, published by the Federation of East European Family History Societies, is reproduced here.

Since much of this information is relevant for all genealogists researching ancestors from Hungary, regardless of ethnicity, this material has been transferred from Appendix 1 ("Current Information Regarding Genealogical Research on Germans from Hungary"), where it appeared in the first edition, to Part I in the second edition.

The indented material is an edited, slightly revised, supplemented and updated version of the material on Hungary in the *Research Guide to German-American Genealogy*. This book contains separate sections for countries to which Hungary ceded territory in 1920 (Austria, Czechoslovakia, Romania, the Soviet Union and Yugoslavia).

HUNGARY (Ungarn)

In discussing Hungarian German genealogical records, we need to keep two important facts in mind.

The first one, which also applies to other countries in southeastern Europe, is that records concerning Germans in modern-day Hungary can be found in three European countries: Hungary, Austria and Germany. What became the Austro-Hungarian Empire in 1867 had been the Austrian Empire before that. Consequently, some of the relevant records are in the Austrian state archives, whose addresses are listed in the AGoFF *Guide*. (Full citation: Arbeitsgemeinschaft ostdeutscher Familienforscher e.V. Herne, *Genealogical Guide to German Ancestors from East Germany and Eastern Europe*, translated by Joachim O. R. Nuthack and Adalbert Goertz, with the English version published by the Verlag Degener & Co., Neustadt/Aisch, Germany, in 1984.) A third edition, popularly known as the *AGoFF-Wegweiser*, was published in 1991. New German and English-language editions are scheduled to be published soon.

The section on Austria has information about the Austrian national archives; especially valuable are the Haus-, Hof- und Staatsarchiv (the chief archives for governmental records) and the Kriegsarchiv (which has extensive military records for the whole empire, beginning in 1740). However, the records pertaining to the German settlers who emigrated to Transylvania and Southern Hungary (Banat, Batschka, Swabian Turkey, etc.) are at the Hofkammerarchiv. All of these are branches of the Austrian National Archives, but are located at different addresses in Vienna. Some of these records or, more likely, copies of them may be in Budapest now as a result of an ongoing exchange and duplication of records among the national libraries of various countries.

Ernest Thode's *Address Book for Germanic Genealogy*, 5th ed. (Baltimore: Genealogical Publishing Co., Inc., 1994) also lists Austrian regional and special archives which may have pertinent information (especially the Burgenländisches Landesarchiv).

Moreover, it is probable that some of the Catholic, Protestant and Jewish religious archives in Austria (AGoFF *Guide*; Thode) also have records pertaining to Hungary. Prior to 1781, Catholic priests kept records for everyone, including Protestants and Jews.

Of course, the voluntary or involuntary departure of Germans from all Eastern European countries, including Hungary, in 1945 and the difficulty of obtaining records from there during the period of Communist rule led to the assembling and reconstructing of a great deal of genealogical data by the refugees in Germany and Austria.

The AGoFF *Guide* has a lengthy section on Southeastern Europe, including the addresses of many organizations and institutions with a greater or lesser interest in genealogy. (The 3rd edition has much more material with respect to individual counties, towns or other small areas.) AGoFF also lists such resources as gazetteers, bibliographies and German cities which have established a special relationship with respect to particular cities in formerly Communist countries from which German refugees came. Much of this information is at least potentially relevant to Hungary.

The second important fact to keep in mind is that Hungarian records may also relate to people in Slovakia and the Carpatho-Ukraine (part of Czechoslovakia during the interwar period); the Vojvodina (formerly an autonomous province of Serbia); Croatia and the northwestern tip of Slovenia; the northwestern third of Romania; and the Burgenland region of Eastern Austria. This is because Hungary historically included all or most of the area surrounded by the Austrian Empire, the Ottoman Turkish Empire, Poland-Lithuania (prior to its partition in 1772-95) and the Russian Empire, although Romania (but only the southern and eastern part of present-day Romania) was recognized as an independent country in 1878.

This area shrank and expanded substantially over the millennium of Hungary's existence, particularly with respect to the waxing and waning of Turkish fortunes in the Balkans. Of course, only a small number of records predating 1526 (when the key battle in the Turkish conquest of Hungary occurred) have been preserved.

The Transylvanian (Siebenbürgen) Saxons were invited by the king of Hungary to settle on his eastern frontier in the twelfth century for defensive reasons. They survived 150 years of Turkish domination before coming under Austrian, then later again Hungarian, administration. Virtually all of the other German colonies in the Balkans, except those close to Austria proper (in Slovenia), were part of the large group usually referred to as the Danube Swabians. They were known as Hungarian-Germans until 1922, because they settled in Southern Hungary in the eighteenth century, after the Turks had been pushed back. But Hungary lost most of this territory after World War I.

Thus these settlements were part of Hungary even before Hungary achieved co-equal imperial status with Austria in 1867, so that pertinent records for all these groups may be found in the national archives in Budapest (and in some other archives) for the period prior to 1919-20, when the map of Europe was drastically redrawn.

In January 1991 the Hungarian National Archives provided me with information relative to German-American genealogical research (but valid for other groups also), which I copied, summarized or paraphrased as follows (with a few comments of my own) in the *Research Guide to German-American Genealogy*:

(1) Archival contents include: church and synagogue registers (births, baptisms, marriages and deaths) which were created in the present territory of Hungary prior to October 1, 1895, when civil registration started; conscription records (lists resembling censuses, not military conscription) pertaining to nobles, serfs, etc.; socage contracts (urbariums), involving feudal tenancy; judicial archives; and military conscription records. About 95% of the parish registers are in good condition. There are some insufficiencies in the Jewish records.

(2) The original church registers are kept by the parishes. Copies of the registers (1828-1895) are kept in the county archives. Civil registers since October 1, 1895, have been kept by local administrative authorities. Requests for information may be sent to any of the three. The LDS Family History Library has microfilms of the pre-1895 registers.

(3) Some of the above records date back to the thirteenth century.

(4) The administrative language of Hungary historically was Latin, except for a short period toward the end of the eighteenth century, when German was used. However, local records in areas of German settlement were in German.

(5) Dr. Ivan Bertényi is the secretary of the Heraldic and Genealogical Society in Budapest, V. Pesti Barnabas u. 1, which is interested in all ethnic groups in Hungary, including Germans. He is primarily a heraldic specialist and speaks German, but not English.

(6) The national and regional or local archives do not undertake genealogical research assignments, but will provide information. (Note: It is conceivable, however, that some arrangements for private research could be made with, or through, the archivists, so a query may be worthwhile.)

(7) For a response to a preliminary inquiry to the Hungarian National Archives, enclose $20 (US) or the equivalent in any convertible currency by international money order or cash transfer to the archives' bank account.

(8) The national archives will respond to letters written in English and to queries specifying a locality if only limited research is required.

(9) Foreign genealogists have access to the archives in Hungary on the same basis as Hungarian researchers.

The AGoFF *Guide* lists the following sources for church records:

(1) *Die Banater Kirchenbücher (Church Books of the Banat)*. An inventory of church records filmed as of 1977, compiled and edited by Josef Schmidt, is at the library of the Institut für Auslandsbeziehungen, Charlottenplatz 17, D-70173 Stuttgart, Germany.

(2) *Inventory of the Hungarian State Archives*, Vol. 72, includes an inventory catalog of microfilm copies of ecclesiastical vital statistics up to October 1, 1895, compiled by Margit Judak of Budapest in 1977.

Thode reports that the synagogue registers of the Hungarian National Archives also include those for the part of the Burgenland region which went to Austria in the boundary changes of 1919-20.

A commercial organization which will do genealogical research and has expertise regarding Hungary is:

> The Genealogical Research Library
> 520 Wellington St.
> London, Ontario N6A 3P9
> Canada

Incidentally, I met Dr. Bertényi in Budapest in 1991 and he referred me to Dr. Imre Reŝs of the Hungarian National Archives, who had worked in Vienna in connection with the exchange of archival documents and with whom I could converse in German.

An inventory of parish registers and other archival material relating to German congregations in Eastern Europe (including Transylvania) which can be found at the Deutsche Zentralstelle für Genealogie in Leipzig has been published since the first edition of this book on Hungary was published. See the bibliography for the full citation.

As far as genealogists with expertise concerning Hungarian research are concerned, two are listed in *Who's Who in Genealogy & Heraldry, 1990*, edited by Mary Keysor Meyer and P. William Filby (available from the publisher at 8944 Madison St., Savage, MD 20763), Claude Andre Donadello (of France) and Jared H. Suess of Salt Lake City, but it does not indicate whether they are available to provide research services. Louis L. Balogh of Provo, Utah, a founding board member of the Federation of East European Family History Societies, is also a Hungarian expert.

The *Resource Guide to East European Genealogy*, first published by the Federation of East European Family History Societies in 1994, which is to be updated biennially, is available from John D. Movius, P.O. Box 4327, Davis, CA 95617-4327. The August 1994 edition lists Douglas P. Holmes, 2811 Elvyra Way #236, Sacramento, CA 95821-5865, who has traveled to Hungary a number of times, as a professional Hungarian genealogist. Dr. Duncan B. Gardiner, C.G., 12961 Lake Ave., Lakewood, OH 44107-1533, and Marilyn K. Sychra, P.I., P.O. Box 23293, Des Moines, IA 50325-3293, are professional genealogists for Slovakia, which was part of pre-World War I Hungary.

Professional translators for Hungarian include John C. Alleman, 204 West 300 North, Salt Lake City, UT 84103-1108; Felix G. Game, 9 Healey Ave. East, Stittsville, ON K2S 1K1, Canada; and Kathy J. Karocki, 124 Esther St., Toledo, OH 43605-1435.

Professional genealogists and/or translators specializing in German and Serbo-Croatian are also listed.

PART II

ADDRESSES OF HUNGARIAN ARCHIVES AS OF JANUARY 1992,

based on information provided by
József Molnár, Chief of the Archives Division of the
Hungarian Ministry of Cultural Affairs and Public Instruction,
to Edward Reimer Brandt,

TOGETHER WITH NOTATIONS CONCERNING SELECTED HOLDINGS OF INDIVIDUAL ARCHIVES,

based on information in the
Guide to the Archives of Hungary

A. National Archives..................................... 40

    1. Central Ministry Responsible for Archival Administration
    2. General Archives
    3. Specialized Archives

B. Local Archives.. 42

    1. City Archives
    2. County (Megye) Archives

C. Archives in Public and Private Institutions............ 49

    1. University Archives
    2. Academies, Scholarly Societies and Specialized Institutes

D. Religious Archives.................................... 51
    1. The Roman Catholic Church
    2. The Reformed (Calvinist) Church
    3. The Evangelical (Lutheran) Church
    4. Other Churches
    5. Jewish Archives

Introductory Notes:

(1) Letters may be written to any of these archives in English or German. The replies, at least from the larger archives, are likely to be in the same language.

(2) The centuries or other dates listed after most of the entries show the period for which archival material has been preserved. Where the detailed description shows material from earlier centuries, it can be presumed that there are only a small number of earlier documents.

(3) The final item under each entry lists the number of running meters (1 meter = 39 inches) of documentary material, thus giving you an accurate idea of the extent of the holdings of each archive.

A. NATIONAL ARCHIVES

1. Central Ministry Responsible for Archival Administration

MŰVELŐDÉSI ÉS KÖZOKTATÁSI MINISZTÉRIUM LEVÉLTÁRI OSZTÁLY
(MINISTRY OF CULTURAL AFFAIRS AND PUBLIC INSTRUCTION, ARCHIVES DIVISION)
H-1250 BUDAPEST, I. Uri utca 54-56 (Pf. 2)
Tel. (1) 156 0372, 156 0939

2. General Archives

MAGYAR ORSZÁGOS LEVÉLTÁR
(HUNGARIAN NATIONAL ARCHIVES)
H-1250 BUDAPEST, I. Bécsi kapu tér 4 (Pf. 3)
Tel. (1) 156 0975, 156 5811, Fax. 156 1858, 1109-1944, 35511 m.

See Part I for detailed description of holdings.

ÚJ MAGYAR KÖZPONTI LEVÉLTÁR
(NEW HUNGARIAN CENTRAL ARCHIVES)
H-1250 BUDAPEST, I. Hess András tér 4 (Pf. 16)
Tel. (1) 175 4367, 155 7201, since 1944, 19377 m.

The New Hungarian National Archives were established in 1970 and sought to collect material from the Communist era. They may be of great value to other researchers, but are largely irrelevant for genealogists. In 1991 an organizational consolidation of the Hungarian National Archives and the New Hungarian National Archives was planned, but they may remain in separate physical facilities, at least for some time. A publication of the new archives, *Archival Manuals: Russian-German-Hungarian Pocket Dictionary of Archival Terminology* (to use the

English translation of the title), may be of particular interest to researchers who know one of these languages.

3. **Specialized Archives**

HADTÖRTÉNELMI LEVÉLTÁR
(ARCHIVES OF MILITARY HISTORY)
H-1250 BUDAPEST, I. Kapisztrán tér 2
Tel. (1) 156 9370, 18th-20th centuries, 6346 m.

Archives established 1919, but has valuable collection of the Turkish period (1441-1789) for areas under Hungarian rule, but Turkish domination. Collection of the Kuruc times (1703-11), nobilitary guards (1760-1850), Royal Guards (1867-1918) and military insurrection (1797-1809). General Headquarters for Hungary (General Kommando für Ungarn) has 1740-1883 records pertaining to settlement of troops, war prisoners, etc. General Military Tribunal (Landes Militär Gericht) has records of bequests, orphans and lawsuits between civil and military persons or organizations for 1802-71. Files of politically unreliable persons for imperial Arad, Pest, Pozsony, Kassa and Nagyvárad military tribunals for the absolutist period (1848-67). (This includes part of contemporary Slovakia and Western Romania.) Records of Honvéd Headquarters (1869-1918) contain data especially on professional soldiers. Short surveys of the archives published in 1959 and 1964.

A KÖZPONTI STATISZTIKAI HIVATAL LEVÉLTÁRA
(ARCHIVES OF THE CENTRAL STATISTICAL OFFICE)
H-1525 BUDAPEST, II. Fényes Elek u. 20 (Pf. 51)
Tel. (1) 115 9240 ext 610, 19th-20th centuries, 4202 m.

Most valuable source (village material of the censuses starting in 1869) not yet in the custody of this archives in 1976.

ORSZÁGOS KÖRNYEZETVÉDELMI ÉS VÍZGAZDÁLKODÁSI LEVÉLTÁR
(NATIONAL ARCHIVES OF THE ENVIRONMENT AND WATER RESOURCE MANAGEMENT)
H-1051 BUDAPEST, V. Arany János u. 25
Tel. (1) 132 7739, 19th-20th centuries, 4419 m.

Not listed in the 1976 *Guide*.

The 1976 *Guide* also listed a small Central Archives of the Trade Unions, H-1075 BUDAPEST, Dózsa György út 68. However, this archives, established in 1970, had records mostly for the Communist era when the unions were not independent of the state. Records of such late date are unlikely to have much genealogical value.

B. LOCAL ARCHIVES

1. City Archives

BUDAPEST FŐVÁROS LEVÉLTÁRA
(BUDAPEST MUNICIPAL ARCHIVES)
H-1350 BUDAPEST, V. Városház u. 9-11 (Pf. 7)
Tel. (1) 117 2033, 17th-20th centuries, 19758 m.

Archives of Buda (Ofen) and Pest date back to 1686; those of Óbuda (Altofen) to 1720. The cities and the archives were consolidated in 1873. Many of the records were destroyed when City Hall burned down in 1945, but others, stored elsewhere, were saved. Section I of the Buda archives contains pre-1945 records; section III contains records of public and private economic enterprises, which may have some limited genealogical value. (Section II deals with the post-1945 period and Section IV with internal affairs.) Óbuda has fragments of records for the "Jewish community," a semi-autonomous organ of the populous Jewry. Mostly government records, including judicial records for some areas outside Budapest. State, religious and private school records. Fragments of guild records, including 8 German butcher guild records, in 1500-1529 guildbook. Many published finding aids for the archives. Publications include a history of Budapest in Hungarian, English and German versions.

2. County (Megye, Komitat) Archives

BÁCS-KISKUN MEGYEI LEVÉLTÁR
(BÁCS-KISKUN COUNTY ARCHIVES)
H-6001 KECSKEMÉT, Kossuth tér 1 (Pf. 77)
Tel. (76) 21 672, 17th-20th centuries, 5950 m.

Few records, since most are in Pest County Archives or in Sremski Karlovic, Serbia. Includes records of former Pest-Pilis-Solt-Kiskun County and 3 districts of former Bács-Bodrog County, which remained in Hungary after 1920. Cadastral survey of Joseph II. Kecskemét city records: tax office (1633-1848), courts (1649-1854), some ancient records back to 1557. Many borough records destroyed. Kalocsa regional court records since 1870s. Various ecclesiastical records (1334-1950). Some family and personal papers back to 1336. Maps of cities (mid-18th century) and villages (ca. 1875-1900).

BARANYA MEGYEI LEVÉLTÁR
(BARANYA COUNTY ARCHIVES)
H-7601 PÉCS, Kossuth Lajos u. 11 (Pf. 392)
Tel. (72) 10 559, 18th-20th centuries, 9434 m.

Records of Pécs (Fünfkirchen) since 1710s. Records of administration under Emperor Joseph II (who sponsored many

German settlements). Despite severe losses, Pécs city archives were considered the largest regional repository before 1945: City Tax Collector's Office (1712-1848), City Treasury of Orphans Court (1783-1848), City Land Register (1750-1848). Regional judicial records, some of national significance. Records of educational institutions: Pécs Episcopal Lyceum of Law (1826-1913), teacher training schools (1870-1948), Cistercian Order's school (1867-1948). Fragmentary guild records. Records of monastery and Pauline and Franciscan Orders. County maps (1749-1886), Pécs city maps (1777-1900), socage maps (1840-1935).

BÉKÉS MEGYEI LEVÉLTÁR
(BÉKÉS COUNTY ARCHIVES)
H-5701 GYULA, Petőfi Sándor tér 3 (Pf. 17)
Tel. (66) 62 173, 18th-20th centuries, 4777 m.

Branch:
H-5630 BÉKÉS, Petőfi u. 4

County records of administration of Joseph II (1786-1790). Assessments of individual localities (1772-1845). Austrian administrative records of Békés-Csanád County (1850-60). Copious material of Wenckheim estate (1854-1944).

BORSOD-ABAÚJ-ZEMPLÉN MEGYEI LEVÉLTÁR
(BORSOD-ABAÚJ-ZEMPLÉN COUNTY ARCHIVES)
H-3501 MISKOLC, Fazekas u. 2 (Pf. 101)
Tel. (46) 44 699, 16th-20th centuries, 6799 m.

Branch:
H-3980 SÁTORALJAÚJHELY, Kossuth tér 5

Borsod, Abaúj-Torna and Zemplén (Semplin) counties united 1949. (Much of the territory in these historic counties is part of Slovakia now.) Most records from former Borsod and Zemplén counties, and city of Miskolc. Valuable old historical records. Judicial and other government records.

CSONGRÁD MEGYEI LEVÉLTÁR
(CSONGRÁD COUNTY ARCHIVES)
H-6720 SZEGED, Dóm tér 1-2 (Pf. 460)
Tel. (62) 21 199, 12th-20th centuries, 11244 m.

Branches:
H-6600 SZENTES, Kossuth tér 1 Tel. 314
(Covers city of Szentes and district of Szentes)
H-6640 CSONGRÁD, Kossuth tér 7 Tel. 31
(Covers city of Csongrád)
H-6309 MAKÓ, Lenin tér 6 Tel. 20
(Covers city of Makó)
H-6800 HÓDMEZŐVÁSÁRHELY, Kossuth tér 1 Tel. 11-122
(Covers city of Hódmezővásárhely)

Former Csanád County had its seat at Makó, near the southern border of present-day Hungary. Portions of Csanád, Arad and Torontál Counties which remained Hungarian after 1920 were combined from 1923 to 1944 (major part of Arad and Torontál became Romanian). Szeged (Szegedin) city records since 1717. Some Makó city records since 1682. (The tiny portion of the Banat, the largest area of Danube Swabian settlement, which remained in Hungary after 1920 was in this area.) Agricultural records of Csanád Catholic bishopric since 1732. [Hódmezövásárhely was 65% Protestant in 1900, according to *Meyers Kleines Konversations-Lexikon*.]

FEJÉR MEGYEI LEVÉLTÁR
(FEJÉR COUNTY ARCHIVES)
H-8001 SZÉKESFEHÉRVÁR, István tér 2-3 (Pf. 52)
Tel. (22) 12 123, 18th-20th centuries, 4540 m.

Branch:
   H-2401 DUNAUJVÁROS, Lenin tér 1 (Pf. 210) Tel. 18-197

Records of Turkish era (1543-1688) in Komaróm, Veszprém, Pest and Györ counties. 5-volume history of county published 1896-1901. Almost complete county records of 1692-1848 (courts, taxes, etc.). Pre-1904 orphans' court records. Property records. Most village records begin in the early 20th century, but those for the city of Székesfehérvár (Stuhlweißenburg) in 1688. Collection of cadastral deeds. Registers of religious schools (1874-1944) and public school of the Pauline-Cistercian Order (1776-1948). Incomplete guild papers (1702-1872). Many ecclesiastical records. Records of aristocratic (including the Hapsburgs) and some bourgeois families. Personal papers of craftsmen, teachers, etc. (1175-1944).

GYÖR-MOSON-SOPRON MEGYEI LEVÉLTÁR
(GYÖR-MOSON-SOPRON COUNTY ARCHIVES)
H-9002 GYÖR, Liszt Ferenc u. 13 (Pf. 36)
Tel. (96) 12 424, 12th-20th centuries, 10078 m.

Branch:
   H-9200 MOSONMAGYARÓVÁR, Városház u. 4 Tel. 16-539
   (Covers city of Mosonmagyaróvár and district of Mosonmagyaróvár)

1976 *Guide* lists Archives # 1 at Györ (Raab) and Archives No. 2 at Sopron (Ödenburg), which have been combined since then. Györ-Sopron County established 1950. Archives # 1 included ecclesiastical records which were continuous since 1534. Records pertaining to tax collector's office, socage matters, orphanages, inquests and attestations. Moson County abolished and combined with Györ in 1923. Valuable records for the Austrian Burgenland area (which formerly belonged to Hungary). After the Turks had largely depopulated the area in the 16th and 17th centuries, mostly German and Croatian settlers replaced the former Hungarian population. County surveys of national censuses (1700, 1713, 1720), socage and land register records (1705-1871). Records of the Győr Regional Superintendance of Schools (1776-1878) embrace all of Transdanubia. Győr Cathedral Chapter Archives contain valuable records for the former Győr, Komárom and Poszony counties (much of this territory is now in Slovakia) and occasionally for other parts of Transdanubia. Archives # 2 were known as the Sopron State Archives until 1968. 1921 plebiscite resulted in transfer of part of this territory to Austria. Nearly 4,000 pre-1500 records published. Many German names listed in the description of contents. Extensive state, church school and convent records. This archives (the closest one to Vienna) suffered little war damage. Publications on the contents of the archives.

HAJDÚ-BIHAR MEGYEI LEVÉLTÁR
(HAJDÚ-BIHAR COUNTY ARCHIVES)
H-4001 DEBRECEN, Piac u. 20 (Pf. 39)
Tel. (52) 11 005, 16th-20th centuries, 5332 m.

Debrecen archives, with city records dating back to 1294, include Turkish records. Assessments and cadastral surveys (1850-1950). Records of Debrecen Chief Inspectorate of Schools (1844-1944) for five former counties, including Szatmár (Sathmar), where there was a German settlement. Socage court records (1856-1872) dealing with land ownership. Records of numerous institutions of middle level (i.e., secondary) education, including public, Catholic, Reformed and specialized schools. Records of Printing House of the Transtibiscan Reformed Church (1794-1948) and Debrecen Convent of the Pious Fathers (1693-1950). Published ethnographic and other maps of 18th-20th centuries. Numerous published descriptions of archival material.

HEVES MEGYEI LEVÉLTÁR
(HEVES COUNTY ARCHIVES)
H-3301 EGER, Lenin u. 140 (Pf. 228)
Tel. (36) 20 164, 16th-20th centuries, 4910 m.

About 65% of material in Hungarian, 35% in German or Latin. Valuable pre-1526 charter collection. Material for Turkish-occupied parts of 3 former counties. Eger (Erlau) had a bishopric (later archbishopric) since conversion to Christianity. Records of numerous schools. Records of Eger Inland Revenue Office, Land Survey Directorate, and County Inspectorate of Schools. Eger guild records, 13th-19th centuries. Historical data on one fifth of Hungary since the days of early feudalism. Maps of settlements since mid-18th century. Several publications of archival records, including socage records.

JÁSZ-NAGYKUN-SZOLNOK MEGYEI LEVÉLTÁR
(JÁSZ-NAGYKUN-SZOLNOK COUNTY ARCHIVES)
H-5001 SZOLNOK, Keskeny János u. 40-42 (Pf. 51)
Tel. (56) 41 404, 16th-20th centuries, 5447 m.

Jász-Nagykun-Szolnok County created in 1876. World War II wreaked havoc to records. Records of 5 villages begin in the 17th century. Records of 3 Reformed schools and one public school. Records of Szolnok Franciscan Convent (1601-1943). List of archival groups and manuscripts published in 1974-75.

KOMÁROM-ESZTERGOM MEGYEI LEVÉLTÁR
(KOMÁROM-ESZTERGOM COUNTY ARCHIVES)
H-2501 ESZTERGOM, Vörösmarty u. 7 (Pf. 51)
Tel. (33) 11 095, 17th-20th centuries, 5117 m.

About half of pre-1918 Esztergom and Komárom counties (area north of the Danube) now in Slovakia. Counties united, separated and reunited since then. Historic Komárom County records in Nitra Státny Archives in Slovakia. Archives of former Royal City of Komárom (Komorn) now in Komárno, Slovakia. Oldest records (1225-1882) are those of Esztergom (Gran) Cathedral Chapter Archives (taken over in 1950), which include much information about Slovakia. Hundreds of pre-1526 records. Valuable 19th-century cadastral survey. School registers of Esztergom Benedictines and other records of Tata Piarists. Hungarian journal of the Esztergom urban millers' guild since 1702.

NÓGRÁD MEGYEI LEVÉLTÁR
(NÓGRÁD COUNTY ARCHIVES)
H-3100 SALGÓTARJÁN, Bem u. 6
Tel. (32) 13 801, 16th-20th centuries, 3042 m.

Branch:
H-2660 BALASSAGYARMAT, Köztársaság tér (Tel. 7-15)
(Covers city of Balassagyarmat and the urban and district organs in its territory from the beginning up to the present)

Large part of the historical county belongs to Slovakia now, so there is important source material about Hungarian villages there. Archives suffered from Turkish wars and several changes of location. Judicial records. Administrative records, including those of the tax collector (1696-1848), include significant national and county conscriptions. Elementary school rolls of ca. 1900, going back to 1834 for Catholic school. Fragments of guild records (18th-19th centuries). Fragmentary records of Szécsény Franciscan Convent (1600-1743). Papers of non-aristocratic landowners, including those of the Schrecker family. Post-1867 land charting, cadastral works and maps. Numerous publications dealing with contents of archives.

PEST MEGYEI LEVÉLTÁR
(PEST COUNTY ARCHIVES)
H-1364 BUDAPEST, V. Semmelweis u. 6 (Pf. 30)
Tel. (1) 117 6297, 17th-20th centuries, 13831 m.

Branch:
NAGYKŐRÖS SECTION OF THE PEST COUNTY ARCHIVES
H-2751 NAGYKŐRÖS, Hősök tere 4-5 (Pf. 52) Tel. 492
(Covers cities of Cegléd and Nagykőrös and district of Cegléd)

Dominated by Turks, 1541-1686. Administrative and judicial organs continued to work in neighboring Nógrád (Neograd) County. Scattered Turkish records. Duplicate religious registers after 1828, civil registers after 1895. Most 19th century censuses and village records of former Pest-Pilis-Solt-Kiskun County (1876-1949) destroyed by amateurish selection of records to be kept. Registers and lists of Pest-Pilis-Solt County materials (1229-1876) facilitate research, though much was decimated in the Turkish wars. Budapest Region Inland Revenue Office and Budapest Region Chief School Inspectorate Records for 1884-1944. Fragments of judicial records, including those pertaining to political prisoners (1863-1944) at Vács Penal Institute. Excellent records of Nagykőrös Public School (1846-1947). Fragmentary guild records. Ecclesiastical records of Vác Chapter, 17th-20th centuries. Quite a few publications dealing with archival material.

SOMOGY MEGYEI LEVÉLTÁR
(SOMOGY COUNTY ARCHIVES)
H-7401 KAPOSVÁR, Rippl Rónai tér 1 (Pf. 91)
Tel. (82) 14 347, 18th-20th centuries, 7416 m.

Records suffered little war damage, but great damage from poor selection of records to be kept. Records of county tax collectors (1691-1848). Almost complete collection of 1767 records regarding regulation of villein socage. Court records (urbarial, 1850-60; civil and criminal processes, 1872-1944). Records of Mernye estate of Custodiate of Pious Fathers (1769-1950). Several publications regarding archival holdings.

SZABOLCS-SZATMÁR-BEREG MEGYEI LEVÉLTÁR
(SZABOLCS-SZATMÁR-BEREG COUNTY ARCHIVES)
H-4400 NYÍREGYHÁZA, Benczúr tér 21
Tel. (42) 11 013, 16th-20th centuries, 3528 m.

Separate counties until 1950. Continuous series of Szabolcs County records from the middle of the 16th century, especially relating to county self-government (judicial and administrative records, tax assessments and popular conscriptions). After 1837 Slovak settlers created a unique privileged civic town administration in Nyíregyháza, but records suffered from damage by carelessness. Nyírbátor Franciscan Convent records (1717-1948). 18th and 19th-century maps concerning settlement and possession of land. Pre-1849 records have indices to subjects, places and names, as well as calendars (registers containing extracts of records). List of archival groups was in the process of publication in 1976. [Most of Szatmár County, where there were German settlements, became part of Romania after World War I, but a few German villages remained in Hungary.]

TOLNA MEGYEI LEVÉLTÁR
(TOLNA COUNTY ARCHIVES)
H-7101 SZEKSZÁRD, Béla tér 1 (Pf. 33)
Tel. (74) 11 718, 18th-20th centuries, 5373 m.

County depopulated by a century and a half of Turkish rule. Considerable World War II damage to records. Mostly county, district and village administrative and legal records. Language of journals of nobilitary assemblies was Latin (1696-1787, 1790-1806), German (1787-89) and Hungarian (after 1807). Pre-1848 conscriptions depict population, taxation, etc. Extensive private Antal Egyed conscription of 1829 (22 questions) for three-fourths of the villages. Records of National Inspectorate of Silk Culture include records for Slovakia, Romania (Transylvania) and Croatia. Several archival publications (list of manuscript maps, list of archival groups, basic inventories, manuscript finding aids).

VAS MEGYEI LEVÉLTÁR
(VAS COUNTY ARCHIVES)
H-9701 SZOMBATHELY, Hefele Menyhért u. 1 (Pf. 78)
Tel. (94) 13 265, 13th-20th centuries, 7732 m.

Branch:
    H-9731 KŐSZEG, Jurisich tér 2 (Pf. 23)
    (covers the area of this city)

Records of Szombathely (Steinamanger) borough since early 17th century. Records of Vasvár Collegial Chapter (1578-1777); then it became a bishopric. Socage records for economic history. Boundary surveys. Cadastral Survey Inspectorate records significant for history of settlement. Records of schools, especially Jesuit-founded Kőszeg (Güns) school (from 1689) and Szombathely secondary school (from 1793). Papers of 47 guilds start at the beginning of the 17th century. Vasvár-Szombathely Cathedral Chapter records important. Medieval records. Continuous journals since 1543 contain valuable data for East Austrian (Burgenland) and Northeastern Slovenian (Prekmurje) areas. Archives of

estates of monks of the Szentgotthárd (Sankt-Gotthard)
Cistercian Abbey have medieval documents and rich socage
data. Kőszeg City (Lábasház) records since the 13th
century valuable for the history of Western Transdanubia;
continuous journals since 1572. List of archival groups
published in 1969.

VESZPRÉM MEGYEI LEVÉLTÁR
(VESZPRÉM COUNTY ARCHIVES)
H-8201 VESZPRÉM, Vár u. 1 (Pf. 152)
Tel. (80) 28 411, 17th-20th centuries, 6435 m.

World War II wreaked havoc to records. Nobilitary assembly
records (1602-1848) include socage records, conscriptions,
testimonies, border surveys and records on orphans. Only
fragments of school and tax records. Some records of
guilds and vine-growing communities. Most medieval
documents come from Veszprém (Wesprim) Cathedral Chapter
(1214-1870), Zirc-Pilis-Pászto-Szentgotthárd United
Cistercian Abbey at Zirc (1295-1950) and Tihany Abbey of
the Benedictine Order of Pannonhalma (1373-1931). Over 600
maps (18th-20th centuries). Several publications,
including list of archival groups published in 1973.

ZALA MEGYEI LEVÉLTÁR
(ZALA COUNTY ARCHIVES)
H-8901 ZALAEGERSZEG, Széchenyi tér 3 (Pf. 110)
Tel. (92) 12794, 16th-20th centuries, 6069 m.

Records of Zalavár Convent. Records of those parts of
Veszprém County which belonged to Zala until 1949.
Assessments according to villages almost complete from 1776
to 1847. Orphans' court records destroyed. Records of
Kesthely borough (1715-1949). Cadastral acts of 3 district
courts between 1861 and 1935. Complete sets of registers
for Keszthely Premonstratensian (1772-1848), Nagykanisza
Piarist (1765-1948) and Nagykanisza State Higher Elementary
Boys School (1872-1948). Fragments of guild records since
1648. Zalavár and Kapornak Abbey records since 1763. List
of archival groups (published 1970) and other publications.

C. ARCHIVES IN PUBLIC AND PRIVATE INSTITUTIONS

There is a short description of special archives, which
included specialized state archives and ecclesiastical
archives, in the 1976 *Guide*, but university archives are not
specifically listed.

1. University Archives

EÖTVÖS LORÁND TUDOMÁNYEGYETEM LEVÉLTÁRA
(ARCHIVES OF LORÁND EÖTVÖS UNIVERSITY)
H-1083 BUDAPEST, VIII. Kun Béla tér 2
Tel. (1) 133 4160, 17th-20th centuries, 619 m.

ÁLLATORVOSTUDOMÁNYI EGYETEM LEVÉLTÁRA
(ARCHIVES OF THE UNIVERSITY OF VETERINARY SCIENCE)
H-1078 BUDAPEST, VII. Landler Jenő u. 2
Tel. (1) 122 0849, 18th-20th centuries, 77 m.

ERDÉSZETI ÉS FAIPARI EGYETEM LEVÉLTÁRA
(ARCHIVES OF THE UNIVERSITY OF FORESTRY AND WOOD INDUSTRY)
H-9401 SOPRON, Bajcsy-Zsilinszky u. 4
Tel. (99) 11 100, 19th-20th centuries, 519 m.

MISKOLCI EGYETEM LEVÉLTÁRA
(MISKOLC UNIVERSITY ARCHIVES)
H-3515 MISKOLC, Egyetemváros
Tel. (46) 66 111, 19th-20th centuries, 332 m.

PANNON AGRÁRTUDOMÁNYI EGYETEM KÖZPONTI LEVÉLTÁRA
(CENTRAL ARCHIVES OF THE PANNONIAN AGRICULTURAL UNIVERSITY)
H-8361 KESZTHELY, Deák Ferenc u. 16
Tel. 12 330, 19th-20th centuries, 131 m.

BUDAPESTI KÖZGAZDASÁGTUDOMÁNYI EGYTEM LEVÉLTÁRA
(ARCHIVES OF THE BUDAPEST UNIVERSITY OF POLITICAL ECONOMY)
H-1093 BUDAPEST, IX. Vámház tér 8
Tel. (1) 118 6855, 19th-20th centuries, 320 m.

2. Academies, Scholarly Societies and Specialized Institutes

A MAGYAR TUDOMÁNYOS AKADÉMIA LEVÉLTÁRA
(ARCHIVES OF THE HUNGARIAN ACADEMY OF SCIENCES)
H-1051 BUDAPEST, V. Roosevelt tér 9
Tel. (1) 138 2344 ext 143, 20th century, 1823 m.

Academy established 1825. Records valuable mostly for scientific history. Several archival publications.

SEMMELWEIS ORVOSTÖRTÉNETI MÚZEUM, KÖNYVTÁR ÉS LEVÉLTÁR
(SEMMELWEIS MUSEUM, LIBRARY AND ARCHIVES OF MEDICAL HISTORY)
H-1013 BUDAPEST, I. Apród u. 1-3
Tel. (1) 175 3533, 19th-20th centuries, 566 m.

Important mostly for records of medical and, to a lesser extent, pharmaceutical associations (many extinct).

D. RELIGIOUS ARCHIVES

1. **The Roman Catholic Church**

ESZTERGOMI PRÍMÁSI LEVÉLTÁR + AZ ESZTERGOMI FŐKÁPTALAN
   LEVÉLTÁRA
(ESZTERGOM PRIMATIAL ARCHIVES + ESZTERGOM CATHEDRAL CHAPTER
   ARCHIVES)
H-2501 ESZTERGOM, Mindszenty tér 2 (Pf. 25)
Tel. (33) 11 288, 12th-20th centuries, 2835 m.

Archbishopric of Esztergom was founded by the first
Hungarian king, St. Stephen, and exercised rights over the
whole Catholic church in Hungary. It also played a leading
role in public life. When the archbishopric fled from the
Turks, it removed its material to Nagyszombat (Tirnau or
Tyrnau), now Trnava, Slovakia. Archbishopric and archives
returned to Esztergom in 1820. Many old documents, going
back to 1138. 19th and 20th century domanial records and
duplicate registers. Excellent contemporary index to
persons, places and subjects up to 1799. Socage books,
donation books, judicial registers, etc., up to 1793.
Domanial Court, Esztergom Seminary and Primatial Court
Christian records. Guide to archives published in 1964.

The 1976 *Guide* listed separate Archives of the Esztergom
Cathedral Chapter, since merged with those of the
archbishopric. These contained records of grants, tithes
and taxation. Published inventory only for early records
up to 1349.

KALOCSAI ÉRSEKI LEVÉLTÁR + A KALOCSAI FŐKÁPTALAN LEVÉLTÁRA
(KALOCSA ARCHIEPISCOPAL ARCHIVES + KALOCSA ARCHDIOCESAN
   CHAPTER ARCHIVES)
H-6301 KALOCSA, Szentháromság tér 1 (Pf. 29)
Tel. Kalocsa 51, 18th-20th centuries, 810 m.

Archbishopric founded by St. Stephen about 1000 A.D. Fell
into Turkish hands in 1529. Records begin in 1691.
Records of parishes (from 1724) and copies of registers.
Separate archival groups for the Court Christian, the
seminary, the public school, the inspectorate of schools,
the Teachers' House, the St. Augustine Association, the
institute for female teachers of religion and the diocesan
savings bank. Socage records, conscriptions, cadastral
maps, etc., are continuous since the mid-18th century.

In 1976 the Kalocsa Archdiocesan Chapter Archives were
listed separately. The chapter was reorganized in 1735
after the Tirkish occupation. Records include public and
charitable gifts, papers on bequests, patrimonial court,
socage redemption, cadastral sheets, etc.

EGRI ÉRSEKI LEVÉLTÁR
(EGER ARCHIEPISCOPAL ARCHIVES)
H-3301 EGER, Széchenyi u. 1 (Pf. 80)
Tel. (36) 13 259, Fax. (36) 20508, 16th-20th centuries, 620 m.

Bishopric of Eger founded in 1009-1010. From the 13th century on, 10 counties in the Northeast region belonged to it; later, 3 more. Eger fell to the Turks in 1596, when bishop and chapter moved to Kassa (Košice, Slovakia), then in 1613 to Jászó (in pre-World War I Abaúj-Torna County), back to Kassa in 1649, returning to Eger in the 1690s. In 1804 bishoprics of Kassa and Szatmár were formed from parts of Eger, which became a metropolitan diocese, responsible for 3 counties and parts of a 4th. Much data for the 1600-1804 period on Kassa and Szatmár (which includes parts of Slovakia and Romania today) remains in Eger. After 1805 there was a separate file for each priest, parish and subject. Series of registers (1690-1805), personal and parish records, records of schools, monks, nuns, canonical visitations (1745-1831), Court Christian (1650-1923), Diocesan Inspectorate of Schools (1850-1948), Eger Franciscan Convent (1690-1900) and Eger Convent of Mary Ward's Nuns (1900-48). Finding aids published in 1957.

GYŐRI PÜSPÖKI LEVÉLTÁR + GYŐRI KÁPTALANI LEVÉLTÁR
(GYŐR EPISCOPAL ARCHIVES + GYŐR CATHEDRAL CHAPTER ARCHIVES)
H-9002 GYŐR, Káptalandomb 1 (Pf. 60)
Tel. (96) 13 255, Fax. (96) 13 256, 13th-20th centuries, 552 m.

Győr occupied by Turks, 1594-98. 1976 *Guide* lists Győr Episcopal Archives as having records of civil lawsuits involving testaments and a few ecclesiastical probate cases; and lists of pupils of Győr seminary. Many records destroyed as a result of the Turkish approach and Napoleon's 1809 siege. Many records transferred to Szombathely diocese in 1777.

Győr Cathedral Chapter Archives had records of Győr Orphans' Home and Foundation and Teachers' Pension Institute (18th-20th centuries). Also records of seigneurial courts involving lawsuits of feudal jurisdiction (18th-19th centuries).

HAJDÚDOROGI GÖRÖGKATOLIKUS PÜSPÖKI LEVÉLTÁR
(HAJDÚDOROG GREEK CATHOLIC EPISCOPAL ARCHIVES)
H-4401 NYÍREGYHÁZA, Bethlen Gábor u. 5 (Pf. 60)
Tel. (42) 17 397, 19th-20th centuries, 49 m.

A Hungarian Greek Catholic diocese was established only in 1912. Oldest records of the vicariate date back to 1878, but the records deal largely with church administration. Some financial records may have incidental genealogical value.

PÉCSI PÜSPÖKI LEVÉLTÁR
(PÉCS EPISCOPAL ARCHIVES)
H-7601 PÉCS, Szent István tér 23 (Pf. 113)
Tel. (72) 14 224, 18th-20th centuries, 336 m.

Records of Diocesan Inspectorate of Schools (1878-1948) relating to teachers. Post-1720 dispensations, testaments, population censuses, lawsuits of the Court Christian, episcopal registers and duplicates.

PÉCSI KÁPTALANI LEVÉLTÁR
(PÉCS CATHEDRAL CHAPTER ARCHIVES)
H-7621 PÉCS, Szent István tér 14
Tel. (72) 13 565, 18th-20th centuries, 170 m.

In 1543, during the Turkish occupation, an effort was made to save the records by transporting them to Pozsony (Preßburg), which is now Bratislavia, Slovakia, but only a few were saved. Records of Pécs Seminary and Theological High School (1747-1950). Collection of 100 maps of church estates. Index to archives published in 1830.

SZEGED-CSANÁDI PÜSPÖKI LEVÉLTÁR + SZEGED-CSANÁDI KÁPTALANI
    LEVÉLTÁR
(SZEGED-CSANÁD EPISCOPAL ARCHIVES + ARCHIVES OF THE SZEGED-
    CSANÁD CATHEDRAL CHAPTER)
H-6701 SZEGED, Aradi vértanúk tere 2 (Pf. 178)
Tel. (62) 11 932, 19th-20th centuries, 570 m.

1976 *Guide* lists the Csanád Episcopal Archives, which were relocated from Timişoara (Romania) to Szeged (Szegedin) after the former locality was separated from Hungary after World War I. Records of 62 parishes which remained in Hungary for 1873-1960.

SZÉKESFEHÉRVÁRI PÜSPÖKI LEVÉLTÁR + SZÉKESFEHÉRVÁRI KÁPTALANI
    LEVÉLTÁR
(SZÉKESFEHÉRVÁR EPISCOPAL ARCHIVES + SZÉKESFEHÉRVÁR CATHEDRAL
    CHAPTER ARCHIVES)
H-8000 SZÉKESFEHÉRVÁR
Tel. (22) 11 490, 18th-20th centuries, 414 m.

Bishopric of Székesfehérvár (Stuhlweißenburg) created in 1777 (formerly part of Veszprém). Episcopal archives have records of Court Christian and Diocesan Inspectorate of Schools. Also duplicate parish registers and records pertaining to non-Catholics.

Cathedral Chapter archives have records on schools, instruction of priests, patrimonial court records (1801-1842), tithes of Fehérvár, socage conscriptions, and records of several Catholic women's and youth organizations.

SZOMBATHELYI PÜSPÖKI LEVÉLTÁR + SZOMBATHELYI KÁPTALANI
   LEVÉLTÁR
(SZOMBATHELY EPISCOPAL ARCHIVES + SZOMBATHELY CATHEDRAL
   CHAPTER ARCHIVES)
H-9701 SZOMBATHELY, Berzsenyi Dániel tér 3 (Pf. 41)
Tel. (94) 12 056, 13th-20th centuries, 455 m.

   Turks driven out of this area in 1699. Szombathely
   Episcopal Archives have church education records, some of
   national significance. Cemetery and patronage records.
   The Catholic press. Records of canonical visitations
   (1698-1837), the Court Christian, dispensations (1856-1869)
   and elementary schools (1857-1948).

   Szombathely Cathedral Chapter Archives (referred to as
   Vasvár-Szombathely in 1976, since the archives of the
   collegiate chapter were at Vasvár (Eisenburg) from the 13th
   to the 16th century) include 17th century records relating
   to villeins, socage dues, lawsuits, testaments, and
   canonical visitations (1713-1815). Also records of
   activities of religious associations and ecclesiastical
   institutions like the diocesan press.

VÁCI PÜSPÖKI LEVÉLTÁR + VÁCI KÁPTALANI LEVÉLTÁR
(VÁC EPISCOPAL ARCHIVES + VÁC CATHEDRAL CHAPTER ARCHIVES)
H-2601 VÁC, Migazzi Kristóf tér 1 (Pf. 167)
Tel. (27) 11 124, 18th-20th centuries, 367 m.

   Reports on the parishes in the 1560s (during the Turkish
   period). Journals of canonical visitations (1673-1892)
   include population records (1712-1856), conscriptions of
   parish revenues (1700-1855), ecclesiastical censuses (1769-
   1920), and imperial conscriptions of parishes and pastors
   (1782-88). Probate records (1710-1947). Records of the
   episcopal seminary (1720-1946), admission to the seminary
   (1760-1920), the Institute for Deaf and Dumb (1900-26), Vác
   Public School (1898-1931) and various religious
   corporations (18th century). Records on Catholic, non-
   Catholic and public schools, and their teachers (1736-
   1948).

   Very little description of the small Vác Cathedral
   Archives, but some records go back to 1700.

VESZPRÉMI PÜSPÖKI LEVÉLTÁR + VESZPRÉMI KÁPTALANI LEVÉLTÁR
(VESZPRÉM EPISCOPAL ARCHIVES + VESZPRÉM CATHEDRAL CHAPTER
   ARCHIVES)
H-8201 VESZPRÉM, Vár u. 16 (Pf. 109)
Tel. (80) 26 088, 11th-20th centuries, 55 m.

   Episcopal archives have 14 volumes of canonical visitations
   (1745-1755), with socio-economic material on the entire
   diocese, including non-Catholics.

Chapter archives suffered great damage in 1381 fire, but records survived the Turkish period by being removed to Sopron in 1544, then relocated in Veszprém in 1630. Records of estates, jurisdiction of the chapter, foundations, conscriptions and 18th-19th century maps. Survey of archives published in 1930.

BENCÉS FŐAPÁTSÁGI LEVÉLTÁR
(ARCHIVES OF THE BENEDICTINE ARCHABBEY)
H-9090 PANNONHALMA, Vár 1
Tel. (96) 70 027, Fax. (96) 70 011, 11th-20th centuries, 180 m.

This may be the oldest, essentially complete archives in the country, with material dating back to about 1100. It withstood the ravages of the Mongols, the Turks and both World Wars with little damage. However, its records seem to be important only for historical research, with little genealogical material.

FERENCES LEVÉLTÁR
(FRANCISCAN ARCHIVES)
H-1024 BUDAPEST, Mártirok útja 23
Tel. (1) 135 8594, 13th-20th centuries, 44 m.

Records for 15 convents since 1730 valuable for local history, but of little genealogical significance.

PIARISTA LEVÉLTÁR
(PIARIST ARCHIVES)
H-1444 BUDAPEST, Mikszáth Kálmán tér 1 (Pf. 266)
Tel. (1) 138 2211, 17th-20th centuries, 240 m.

Significant historical and some financial records, but little for the genealogist.

The 1976 *Guide* also listed the Sopron Collegiate Chapter Archives, H-9400 SOPRON, Orsolya tér 4, which had socage records, conscriptions of holdings and of villeins, as well as their petitions and complaints, corvée lists, ecclesiastical records (1727-1909), and the private papers of Baron Barco, including estate maps, records on mines in Transylvania and a copy of the journal of the Transylvanian Diet of 1794-95. It is unclear where the records of this small archive, which had no archivist in 1976, are now.

2. <u>The Reformed (Calvinist) Church</u>

A MAGYARORSZÁGI REFORMÁTUS EGYHÁZ ZSINATI LEVÉLTÁRA
(SYNODAL ARCHIVES OF THE REFORMED CHURCH OF HUNGARY)
H-1091 BUDAPEST, Kálvin tér 8
Tel. (1) 117 6478, 18th-20th centuries, 803 m.

Mostly administrative church records, but some on old age pension fund and the institute for protecting widows and orphans. Very brief survey of records published as an article.

A DUNAMELLÉKI REFORMÁTUS EGYHÁZKERÜLET LEVÉLTÁRA
(ARCHIVES OF THE DANUBIAN REFORMED CHURCH DISTRICT)
H-1092 BUDAPEST, Ráday u. 28
Tel. (1) 117 6321, 17th-20th centuries, 575 m.

Historical material since 1204. Archives of more than 100 families, including many prominent ones, with some going back to the 13th century. Surveys of archival material have been published.

A DUNÁNTÚLI REFORMÁTUS EGYHÁZKERÜLET LEVÉLTÁRA
(ARCHIVES OF THE TRANSDANUBIAN REFORMED CHURCH DISTRICT)
H-8500 PÁPA, Március 15 tér 9
Tel. (89) 24 240, 17th-20th centuries, 450 m.

Suffered major war damage. Mostly administrative records (1583-1952). Records of public schools (1789-1952), the theological academy (1794-1953) and the teachers' training college (1870-1903). Records for 6 dioceses, the oldest going back to 1677. Descriptive article on the archives' records has been published.

A TISZÁNINNENI REFORMÁTUS EGYHÁZKERÜLET LEVÉLTÁRA
(ARCHIVES OF THE CISTIBISCAN REFORMED CHURCH DISTRICT)
H-3950 SÁROSPATAK, Rákóczi u. 1 (Pf. 82)
Tel. (41) 11 057, 17th-20th centuries, 407 m.

Founded in 1735. A number of family archives, with some records dating back to 1270. Guild papers provide indices of dates, places and names. School registers for Sárospatak Reformed College (1617-1847). Records of the academy of law, the teachers' training college, the lyceum, the boarding house and youth associations. Records of Miskolc Reformed Public School (1821-1948). Records of 5 deaneries.

A TISZÁNTÚLI REFORMÁTUS EGYHÁZKERÜLET LEVÉLTÁRA
(ARCHIVES OF THE TRANSTIBISCAN REFORMED CHURCH DISTRICT)
H-4044 DEBRECEN, Kálvin tér 16 (Pf. 201)
Tel. (52) 18 297, 16th-20th centuries, 929 m.

Archives of the Reformed College (1588-1950) include material on progress of students and on boarding houses. Local historical material for 9 dioceses, the oldest documents going back to 1567. Archival survey article published. Archival reference library, microfilms and xerox machine.

3. The Evangelical (Lutheran) Church

EVANGÉLIKUS ORSZÁGOS LEVÉLTÁR
(EVANGELICAL NATIONAL ARCHIVES)
H-1085 BUDAPEST, Üllői út 24
Tel. (1) 114 2009, 16th-20th centuries, 750 m.

Includes records from deaneries outside the present borders of Hungary, which may be especially significant for the Transylvanian Saxons and possibly other non-Magyar ethnic groups. School, orphan and organizational records have some genealogical value. Two published volumes on the holdings of the archives.

A BÉKÉSCSABAI EVANGÉLIKUS GYÜLEKEZET LEVÉLTÁRA
(ARCHIVES OF THE BÉKÉSCSABA EVANGELICAL CONGREGATION)
H-5600 BÉKÉSCSABA, Luther u. 1
Tel. (66) 22 162, 18th-20th centuries, 50 m.

Established in 1718. Fragmentary records concerning schools, orphans and homes for the aged. [There were Slovaks resident in Békéscsaba, according to *Meyers Kleines Konversations-Lexikon*.]

A NYÍREGYHÁZI EVANGÉLIKUS GYÜLEKEZET LEVÉLTÁRA
(ARCHIVES OF THE NYÍREGYHÁZA EVANGELICAL CONGREGATION)
H-4400 NYÍREGYHÁZA, Iskola u. 1
Tel. (42) 11 360, 18th-20th centuries, 17 m.

Contains mostly correspondence. Some death records.

A SOPRONI EVANGÉLIKUS GYÜLEKEZET LEVÉLTÁRA
(ARCHIVES OF THE SOPRON EVANGELICAL CONGREGATION)
H-9400 SOPRON, Templom u. 10
17th-20th centuries, 59 m.

Has birth registers since 1624, marriage registers since 1645 and death registers since 1676. Records on professors and teachers (1648-1872) and orphans (1749-1872). [This could possibly include the Austrian Burgenland, although that is not specified in the *Guide*.]

A SZARVASI EVANGÉLIKUS GYÜLEKEZET LEVÉLTÁRA
(ARCHIVES OF THE SZARVAS EVANGELICAL CONGREGATION)
H-5540 SZARVAS (Pf. 22)
Tel. (67) 13 153, 18th-20th centuries, 34 m.

Records of the minister's office (1734-1972) include registers. Records on aid to widows and orphans (1890-1946) and on the Lutheran orphanage (1917-1962).

4. Other Churches

HAJDÚDOROGI GÖRÖGKATOLIKUS PÜSPÖKI LEVÉLTÁR
(HAJDÚDOROG GREEK CATHOLIC EPISCOPAL ARCHIVES)
H-4401 NYÍREGYHÁZA, Bethlen Gábor u. 5 (Pf. 60)
Tel. (42) 17 397, 19th-20th centuries, 49 m.

A Hungarian Greek Catholic diocese was established in 1912. Oldest records of the vicariate date back to 1878, but the records deal largely with church administration. Some financial records may have incidental genealogical value.

A MAGYARORSZÁGI BAPTISTA EGYHÁZ LEVÉLTÁRA
(ARCHIVES OF THE HUNGARIAN BAPTIST CHURCH)
H-1062 BUDAPEST, Aradi u. 48
Tel. (1) 132 2332, Fax. 131 0194, 19th-20th centuries, 56 m.

Baptist congregations have existed continuously since 1873, but were legally recognized only in 1905. No records of the Anabaptists who settled in Hungary in the 16th and 17th centuries. Fragmentary records of theological institutions, house of charity, home for aged ministers, Bible study groups and youth associations.

A GÖRÖGKELETI SZERB EGYHÁZ LEVÉLTÁRA
(GREEK ORTHODOX SERBIAN EPISCOPAL ARCHIVES)
H-2001 SZENTENDRE, Engels u. 5 (Pf. 22)
Tel. (26) 12 399, 18th-20th centuries, 110 m.

Settlement of Greek Orthodox Serbians fleeing the Turks began in the 14th century. Has pre-1896 parish registers and church school records beginning in 1872.

MAGYARORSZÁGI UNITÁRIUS EGYHÁZ LEVÉLTÁRA
(ARCHIVES OF THE HUNGARIAN UNITARIAN CHURCH)
H-1055 BUDAPEST, Nagy Ignác u. 4
Tel. (1) 111 3094, 19th-20th centuries, 52 m.

Unitarians appeared in the area bordering on Transylvania (now in Romania) and in Baranya County (which is now partly in the Vojvodina) in the late 17th century, but they were annihilated by the Counter-Reformation. There have been Unitarians in Hungary continuously since the second half of the 19th century. Archives gathers data on the 16th and 17th century Unitarian movements. Collection of data, begun in 1953, became an archive in 1961. Registers of numerous congregations, records of extinct associations, and the Unitarian press. Hungarian Unitarian Encyclopedia and a history of the Unitarian church.

5. <u>Jewish Archives</u>

MAGYAR ZSIDÓ LEVÉLTÁR
(HUNGARIAN JEWISH ARCHIVES)
H-1085 BUDAPEST, József körút 27
Tel. (1) 142 1335, 19th-20th centuries, 60 m.

Nearly 50 monographs of Jewish religious communities have been published, based on the archives which almost all communities had, several dating back 200 years. Archival material was largely annihilated during the Nazi period, but records of 6 communities were saved wholly or substantially. With a few exceptions, records of only the 19th and 20th centuries remain. Fragments of 20th century educational and associational records.

APPENDICES, TABLES AND MAPS

These are intended particularly for research on ethnic Germans in contemporary or historic Hungary (although some of the information may also be of value to genealogists with other ethnic backgrounds) and include:

Appendices on
(1) names of selected localities in pre-Trianon Hungary in Hungarian, German and other languages
(2) historic events in Hungary affecting Germans
(3) a select bibliography on researching Germans in Hungary

Statistical tables on
(1) the number of native German-speakers in various regions of historic Hungary
(2) the counties and cities with the largest number of Germans
(Both are based on Prof. Dr. Wilhelm Winkler, *Statistisches Handbuch des gesamten Deutschtums*, published by the Verlag Deutsche Rundschau, Berlin, in 1927.)

Maps of Hungary
(1) before and after World War I
(2) showing current Hungarian counties and cities, identifying those with the largest number of German-speakers in 1910
(3) showing the pre-World War I counties of Hungary

Appendix 1

NAMES OF SELECTED LOCALITIES IN PRE-TRIANON HUNGARY IN HUNGARIAN, GERMAN AND OTHER LANGUAGES

[Note: Names were generally selected because they appeared in the *Guide to the Archives of Hungary*, because they were significant for historic reasons or purposes of orientation, or because German settlements existed in the area. Much more complete lists of names can be found in several of the gazetteers listed in Appendix 3, especially Batowski for those whose research involves non-German ancestors. Some of these localities changed names or were known by more than one name; not all of these are listed in all cases. The various sources were not always completely consistent in spelling names. Remember that the German "ß" is equivalent to "ss."]

HUNGARY

Hungarian	German
Budapest	Budapest, Ofenpest
Buda	Ofen
Óbuda	Altofen
Debrecen	Debrezen, Debreczen
Eger	Erlau
Esztergom	Gran
Győr	Raab
Gyulafehérvár	Karlsburg
Kőszeg	Güns
Mosonmagaróvar, Moson	Wieselburg
Nagykanisza	Groß-Kanisza
Pécs	Fünfkirchen
Sopron	Ödenburg
Szeged	Szegedin
Székesfehérvár	Stuhlweißenburg
Szentgotthárd	Sankt-Gotthard
Szombathely	Steinamanger
Vas, Vasvár	Eisenburg
Veszprém	Wesprim

AUSTRIA (BURGENLAND)

Hungarian	German
Kismarton	Eisenstadt
Nagy-Marton	Mattersdorf
Naszider	Neusiedl am See
Német-Keresztur	Deutschkreutz

SLOVAKIA

Hungarian	German	Slovak
Gölnicbánya	Göllnitz	Gelnica
Igló	Zipser Neudorf	Spišske Nová Ves
Jánosgyaramat	Drechslerhau, Drexlerhau	Janova Lehota
Kassa	Kaschau	Košice
Késmárk	Käsmark	Kežmarok
Komaróm	Komorn	Komárno
Körmöcbánya	Kremnitz	Kremnica
Löcse	Leutschau	Levoča
Nagyszombat	Tyrnau, Tirnau	Trnava
Nemetprona, Felsöpróna	Deutsch-Proben	Nemecké Pravno, Nitrianske Pravno
Nyitra	Neutra	Nitra
Nyitrabánya	Krickerhau	Handlová
Ólubló	Altlublau	Stará L'ubovna
Pálasnagymezö, Nagymezö	Hochwies	Vel'ke Pole
Poprád	Deutschendorf	Poprad
Pozsony	Preßburg	Bratislava
Szepes	Zips	Spiš
Szepesv∇ralya	Kirchdrauf, Kirchdorf	Spišské Podhrahie
Trencsén	Trentschin	Trenčín

(CARPATHO-)UKRAINE

Hungarian	German	Slovak	Ukrainian
Munkács	Munkatsch	Mukačevo	Mukachevo

ROMANIA

Hungarian	German	Romanian
Bakóvár	Bakowa	Bacova
Balázsfalva	Blasendorf	Blaj
Beszterce-Naszod	Bistritz-Naßod (Nösen)	Bistriţa-Năsăud
Brassó	Kronstadt	Braşov
Gyulafehérvár	Karlsburg (Weißenburg)	Alba Iulia
Koloszvár	Klausenburg	Blaj
Lugos	Lugosch	Lugoj
Medges	Mediasch	Mediaş
Nagyenyed	Straßburg	Aiud

Hungarian	German	Romanian
Nagykaroly	Groß-Karol	Carei (Mare)
Nagyszeben	Hermannstadt	Sibiu
Nagyvárad	Großwardein	Oradea
Resizabánya	Reschitz	Reşiţa
Szászsebes	Mühlbach	Sebeş
Szatmár	Sathmar	Satu Mare
Temesvár	Temeschburg, Temeschwar	Timişoara
Zsombolya	Hatzfeld	Jimbolia

SERBIA AND VOJVODINA

Hungarian	German	Serbian
Féhertemplon	Weißkirchen	Bela Crkva
Modos	Modosch	Jaša Tomić
Nagybecskerek	Groß-Betschkerek	Zrenjanin, Velika Beckerek
Nagykikinda	Groß-Kikinda	Velika Kikinda
Nemet-Palánka	Deutsch-Palanka	Bačka-Palanka
Pancsova	Pantschowa	Pančevo
Petervárad	Peterwardein	Petrovaradin
Újverbász	Werbaß	Vrbas
Versecz	Werschetz	Vršac
Zimony	Semlin	Zemun

CROATIA

Hungarian	German	Croatian
Djakóvar	Djakoward	Đakovo, Djakovo
Eszék	Esseg, Essek	Osijek, Osjek
Fiume	Fiume	Rijeka, Reka
Vinkovce (formerly Cibálä)	Winkowcze	Vinkovci
Vukovár	Wukowar	Vukovar
Zágráb	Agram	Zagreb

Sources:
(1) Batowski, Henryk, *Słownik Nazw Miejscowych Europy Srodkowej i Wschodniej XIX i XX Wieku* (Warsaw: Pánstwowe Wydawnictwo Naukowe, 1964)
(2) Gardiner, Duncan B., *German Towns in Slovakia & Upper Hungary: A Genealogical Gazetteer*, 3rd ed. (Lakewood, OH: The Family Historian, 1991)
(3) Michels, John M., *Introduction to the Hungarian-Germans of North Dakota* (Bismarck: Germans from Russia Heritage Society, February 1988)
(4) *Meyers Kleines Konversations-Lexikon*, 6 vols. (Leipzig & Vienna: Bibliographisches Institut, 1908-09)

(5) *National Geographic Atlas of the World* (Washington: National Geographic Society, 1993)
(6) Nuthack, Joachim O. R., and Adalbert Goertz (transl. of AGoFF-Wegweiser, 2nd ed.), *Genealogical Guide to German Ancestors from East Germany and Eastern Europe* (Neustadt/Aisch: Verlag Degener & Co., 1984)
(7) Quester, Erich (comp.), *Wegweiser für Forschung nach Vorfahren aus den ostdeutschen und sudetendeutschen Gebieten sowie aus den deutschen Siedlungsräumen in Mittel-, Ost- und Südosteuropa* (AGoFF-Wegweiser, 3rd ed.) (Neustadt/Aisch: Verlag Degener & Co., 1991)
(8) Steigerwald, Jacob, *Tracing Romania's Heterogeneous Minority from Its Origin to the Diaspora* (Winona, MN: author, 1985)

Appendix 2

DATELINE OF HISTORIC EVENTS IN HUNGARY OF PARTICULAR RELEVANCE FOR RESEARCH ON GERMAN ANCESTORS

Date	Event(s)
896	Magyar tribes from the east conquer Hungary.
997-1038	Reign of St. Stephen, first as duke, then after 1001 as "Apostolic King." Upon advice of his Bavarian-born wife, Gisela, he welcomed the first wave of Germans (monks, preachers, knights, traders and craftsmen), chiefly to strengthen the newly established Christianity and to fight against the pagan chieftain, Koppány, who challenged Stephen's right to rule.
1141-1181	Transylvanian "Saxons" (actually mostly Franks, coming from a strip reaching from Flanders and Brabant to Bavaria and Thuringia, with a concentration from around Luxembourg, causing them to be referred to by scholars as "Mosel Franks") were invited by King Géza II (1141-1163) and his successors to settle along, and defend, Hungary's eastern frontier.
12th & 13th centuries	Germans settled in the Zips (Szepes, Spiš) area at the eastern foot of the Tatra Mountains in order to develop mining.
1211	King Andrew (András) II invited the Teutonic Knights to settle in the Burzenland to plug the gap in his defense line. The Teutonic Knights were soon ordered to leave because of repeated quarrels, but the settlers they brought with them were allowed to stay.
1224	King Andrew II issued the famous "golden patent," the *Andreaneum*, which granted special rights and privileges, including personal freedom, the right to own land and local autonomy, to the Germans living on the *Königsboden* (royal land) around Hermannstadt (now Sibiu) in Transylvania, the Zipser (descended from the Tatra miners) around Nösen, later changed to Bistritz (Bistriţa), and to those in the Burzenland, but this did not apply to Germans living on neighboring noblemen's estates.
1240-1242	Mongol raids destroyed much of the area, especially south of Zips, but resettlement and recovery were rapid.

1421	The Ottoman Turks conquered Brașov (Kronstadt). The Transylvanian Saxons soon formed a *Nationsuniversität* to administer common lands. They also formed a perpetual defensive alliance against mutual enemies with the Hungarian Széklers and the Romanians.
1437	The Turks fail to capture Hermannstadt.
1458-1490	Matthias Corvinus produced Hungary's "golden age," but there were no strong leaders to follow him, thus paving the way for successful Turkish advances.
1522	The Austrian Military Frontier (Zone) was established along the southern and eastern borders with Turkish-controlled territory. It was settled and defended mostly by Slavic and Orthodox citizen-soldiers, with Germans comprising about 4% of the residents. In colloquial Austrian, it was referred to as the *Gränitz* (*Grenz* or border).
1526	The Turks decisively defeated the Hungarians at the Battle of Mohács and took over two-thirds of the country. Since the Hungarian king, Louis II, died in the battle, Ferdinand I of Hapsburg (1526-1564) inherited the Hungarian crown and ruled the western and northern slivers of Hungary. The Transylvanian Saxons managed to retain a degree of local autonomy under vassal rulers. At this time, 80% of the residents of Hungary were ethnic Magyars.
1529	In the first Turkish siege of Vienna, the Turks did not capture the city, but they forced Emperor Ferdinand to pay an annual tribute for continuing to rule Western Hungary.
1545	The Transylvanian Saxons became Lutherans. The Catholic Hapsburgs could not intervene because all the surrounding territory was held by the Turks.
1671	The Tököly conspiracy against the imperial government was one example of Hungarian actions which caused the Hapsburgs to consider the Magyars unruly, which may have contributed to the later decision to settle non-Magyars in the areas won back from the Turks.

1683	General Sobieski (King John III of Poland) led allied troops in a successful defense of Vienna, routing the Turks and turning the historical tide against them.
1686	Budapest was recaptured from the Turks.
1687	The Hapsburgs gained control over much of Transylvania.
1690	Leopold I created a Neo-acquisition Commission to examine claims to land regained from the Turks and to decide what to do about unclaimed land. Many Hungarian lords friendly to the Hapsburgs were happy to accept settlers from anywhere (most of whom were Germans) to redevelop their land.
1692-93	Extensive rights were granted to the residents of the Austrian Military Frontier, cementing their loyalty to the emperor.
1699	The Treaty of Karlowitz ended the war which ousted the Turks from most of Hungary and Croatia. Emperor Leopold I restored the rights of the Transylvanian Saxons, but local Austrian generals who regarded the area as conquered territory and Kuruz raids made life difficult.
1703-1711	The insurrection of Rákóczy represented another conflict between Magyars and the emperor.
1710	The residents of the Austrian Military Frontier were given the responsibility to keep out plagues and epidemics spreading from the southeast, which they did successfully.
1712, 1720	The first Germans were invited by Count Karolyi to settle in the Szatmár (Sathmar in German, Satu Mare in Romanian) region along what is now the border between northwestern Romania and eastern Hungary, following the 1711 Treaty of Satu Mare.
1713	The Pragmatic Sanction stressed the indivisibility of the empire, a theme that dominated Hapsburg policy to the end.
1715	The Hapsburgs agreed to let Hungarian authorities and estates participate in administering the Banat and share in its revenue, but failed to honor the agreements.
1718	The Banat became an Austrian crown province after reconquest ratified by Treaty of Passarovits.

1723	The Hungarian estates accepted the Pragmatic Sanction, which secured the continuity of Hapsburg rule and asked the emperor to send German settlers to repopulate the devastated territories.
1718-1737	The first of the three phases of the "Great Swabian Migration" to the Banat occurred as a colonization effort by Charles VI (1711-1740). Many of these settlers died in subsequent Turkish raids.
1731-1762	Religious refugees from Salzburg and the *Salzkammergut* in Eastern Austria emigrated to Protestant Transylvania.
1740-80	Empress Maria Theresa, who ruled during this period, set up a commission to look into the grievances of Germans living on private domain (i.e., under nobles), whose lot was much worse than that of those who lived under public domain (directly responsible to the monarch). The reforms, which gave these settlers access to the crown, lasted only until 1790.
1743	Germans from the Bad Durlach area in Baden emigrated to Transylvania, which had regained its prosperity by then.
1744-1772	The second phase of the "Swabian" colonization was promoted by Empress Maria Theresa. The settlers apparently came to be known as "Swabians" because they embarked at Ulm in Swabia and sailed down the Danube to their destination. In reality, the largest number came from Lorraine, followed by those from the Trier-to-Mainz area, now the Rhineland-Palatinate.
1748-1881	The Austrian Military Frontier was gradually abolished.
1749-1772	Emigrants from Alsace and the Black Forest area migrated to Transylvania.
1781	The Patent of Tolerance guaranteed religious freedom in Austrian-ruled lands and opened the way for Protestant immigration.
1782-1787	Emperor (Francis) Joseph II (1780-1790) recruited immigrants from southwestern Germany, central Germany and Alsace-Lorraine in the third phase of the "Swabian" migration to the Banat, as well as to the Batschka. It is estimated that 150,000

"Swabians" settled on the territory liberated from the Turks altogether.

1783	Emperor (Francis) Joseph II issued two decrees, which were bound to have negative effects on the Germans in Transylvania. He opened up the area to settlement by non-Germans, making it harder for the Germans to preserve their way of life. He also replaced Latin with German as the official language, causing Hungarian resentment against the Germans which surfaced overtly in the Revolution of 1848-49.
1787	Only 39% of the people of Hungary were ethnic Magyars at this time, due largely to the settlement of Germans, as well as the Slavs and Romanians along the Military Frontier.
1790-1803	The French Revolution caused a small (2,000 persons) emigration to the lower Danubian area, almost all of the migrants coming from Alsace-Lorraine.
1799	The Banat was administratively incorporated into Hungary, although it continued to have a special status.
1848-49	The Europe-wide revolutions of these years had the Transylvania Saxons and the Romanians opposed to the forces led by the Hungarian national hero, Lajos Kossuth, although many of the Germans living near the Military Frontier supported him. The anti-minority actions of the Hungarians led the Germans in Transylvania to opt for Romania, rather than Hungary, after World War I. Budapest was 75% German at this time; most of the towns were also predominantly German. This began to change immediately thereafter. Serfdom was abolished, but this affected few Germans in Hungary.
1849	The Vojvodina (now an autonomous province of the republic of Serbia in what is or was Yugoslavia) was formed from a part of the Military Frontier.
1850	The powers of the more than 300-year-old *Nationsuniversität* of the Transylvanian Saxons were effectively transferred to the church.
1867	The Austro-Hungarian (Dual) Monarchy was established. Magyarization (forced assimilation) of national minorities became the policy of the Hungarian government. This policy was more successful (1) in cities than in rural areas,

where the overwhelming majority of Germans lived, (2) among Catholics than among Protestants, and (3) among the Danube Swabians than among the Transylvanian Saxons (especially among those who aspired to civilian or military government positions, which required assimilation, whereas the Transylvanian Saxons had a long history of local autonomy). The *Andreaneum* of 1224 was annulled.

1870-90	Agricultural production nearly doubled as the population increased. This also meant that there was relatively little new land which could be made arable, so large families had to look for alternatives for their sons.
1873	The cities of Buda (which used to be called Ofen), Óbuda (Altofen) and Pest, on opposite banks of the Danube River, were amalgamated into Budapest.
1886	The first Transylvanian Saxons emigrated to the United States.
1890	A "Saxon bloc" was formed in the Hungarian assembly.
1890-1910	Rapid urbanization took place as the percentage of residents engaged in agricultural pursuits declined from 65% to 40%.
1894-98	Some Germans from Cservenka in the Batschka and from the Banat migrated to Transylvania.
1895	Hungary introduced civil registration of births, deaths and marriages, records which are still complete.
1896	Only one school teaching both German and Hungarian was left in Hungary, compared to 24 in 1868. The same year, Theodor Herzl (1860-1904), a Budapest-born Austrian writer, published *Jewish State*, the foundation of Zionism, but only after he had become convinced that his earlier hope for Jewish assimilation could never be realized.
1900	The population of Budapest was now 85% Magyar, 9% German and 3% Slovak. Jews constituted 23% of the population, considerably more than the total number of Protestants.
1902	The Alliance of Transylvanian Saxons was formed in the United States.

1909-10	This was the first peak of Transylvanian Saxon immigration to the United States.
1914	By now, 20% of the Banat Germans had emigrated.
1914-18	The Austro-Hungarian Empire was allied with Germany in World War I, while Yugoslav, Romanian and Slovak leaders supported the other side.
1918-21	De facto independence by Yugoslavia and Czechoslovakia immediately after the war was officially recognized by the Treaty of Trianon in 1920. Transylvania and two-thirds of the Banat, which contained nearly a million Germans, were transferred to Romania. Half a million came under the rule of Yugoslavia: a few of them from Croatia-Slavonia (not to be confused with Slovenia) and fewer still from Bosnia-Herzegovina, which had been administered by the Austro-Hungarian joint imperial government, but the vast majority of them from the Batschka (Bačka), one-third of the Banat and most of Baranya, in which area they constituted one-quarter of the population. Hungary also ceded a portion of the Burgenland to Austria following a 1921 plebiscite. A Minority Rights Agreement, to be supervised by the League of Nations, was also adopted as part of the peace settlement and applied to all the countries in Southeastern Europe.
1920s	Novi Sad (Neusatz) became the "Swabian capital" of Yugoslavia. Previously, Temesvár (Temeschburg, now Timişoara, Romania) had been the largest center for the whole Danube Swabian area. Laws were much more favorable to the Germans, especially with respect to education, in Romania, Yugoslavia and, to some extent, Czechoslovakia than in Hungary, which Paikert attributes to a desire by these countries to prevent the two largest minorities, Germans and Magyars, from forming an alliance, which might have created serious problems for these states.
ca. 1938	Many German groups in Southeastern Europe became pro-Nazi, as Hitler annexed Austria and the Sudetenland region of Czechoslovakia.
1939-45	World War II found Hungary and Romania joining the Axis in 1940, while Yugoslavia joined the Allies in 1941. Romania suddenly switched sides in 1944, which created problems for the Germans living there. The guerilla operations conducted against the German occupiers by Tito and by

	forces loyal to the king led to ruthless retaliation against innocent civilians by the Nazi authorities. This poisoned what had been good relations between the Yugoslavs and the local Germans. The result was that Yugoslavia was more vehemently anti-German after the war than any other country.
1940-44	Northern Transylvania, the Satu Mare region and southern Slovakia were reincorporated into Hungary as a result of German-Italian arbitration. This was, of course, undone as Soviet forces reached the area.
1944-45	Most adult Germans in Romania were deported to forced labor camps in the Soviet Union. Many died there, but the survivors were released in 1948-51. Romania was the only East European country to allow all its Germans to return and to retain their cultural identity, but only if it was "socialist" in substance.
1945-48	German adults were held in concentration camps in Yugoslavia. Very few stayed in the country thereafter. About half of the Danube Swabians in Hungary were sent to Austria or Germany, when the Allies first authorized Hungary to follow the Polish and Czech precedent of expulsion, but later withdrew their cooperation.
1950s	The heaviest immigration of Danube Swabians to the United States brought the total to a quarter million, concentrated in the Midwest, especially Ohio, but also in New York, Pennsylvania and California.
1956	Soviet troops put down an anti-Communist revolution in Hungary.
1968	The Hungarian government began to adopt liberalizing reforms.
1983-85	Romania began to allow Germans to leave the country and its harsh rule, at first with severe restrictions. Steigerwald estimates that by 1985 only 40% of the Danube Swabians who had lived in Romania were still there. Of those who left, about 75% stayed in Austria or Germany, while the rest moved on to 27 countries, especially Argentina, Australia, Brazil, Canada, France, the United States and Venezuela.
1989	Hungary became the first Communist country to open its borders to the West, allowing many East

Germans to flee to Austria. The collapse of Communism followed almost immediately everywhere.

Chief Sources

1. Paikert, G. C., *The Danube Swabians in Hungary, Rumania and Yugoslavia and Hitler's Impact on Their Patterns* (The Hague: Martinus Nijhoff, 1967)

2. Steigerwald, Jacob, *Tracing Romania's Heterogeneous German Minority from Its Origins to the Diaspora* (Winona, MN: author, 1985) (Address: 355 West Fourth St., Winona, MN 55987, USA)

Other Sources Used

1. Arbeitsgemeinschaft ostdeutscher Familienforscher e.V. Herne (eds.), *Genealogical Guide to German Ancestors in East Germany and Eastern Europe*, 2nd ed., translated by Joachim O. R. Nuthack & Adalbert Goertz (Neustadt/Aisch, Germany: Verlag Degener & Co., 1984)

2. Arbeitsgemeinschaft ostdeutscher Familienforscher e.V. Herne (compiled by Erich Quester), *Wegweiser für die Forschung nach Vorfahren aus den ostdeutschen und sudetendeutschen Gebieten sowie aus den deutschen Siedlungsgebieten in Ost- und Südosteuropa (AGoFF-Wegweiser)*, 3rd ed. (Neustadt/Aisch, Germany: Verlag Degener & Co., 1991)

3. Bellingham, Mary, Edward R. Brandt, Kent Cutkomp, Kermit Frye and Karen Whitmer, *Research Guide to German-American Genealogy* (St. Paul: German Interest Group [now Germanic Genealogy Society], 1991) (Address: P.O. Box 16312, St. Paul, MN 55116, USA)

4. Macartney, C. A., *A History of Hungary, 1929-1945*, Part I (New York: Frederick A. Praeger, 1956)

5. *Meyers Kleines Konservations-Lexikon*, 6 vols. (Leipzig & Vienna: Bibliographisches Institut, 1908-09)

6. Michels, John M., *Introduction to the Hungarian-Germans of North Dakota* (Bismarck: Germans from Russia Heritage Society, February 1988) (Address: 1008 East Central Ave., Bismarck, ND 58501, USA)

7. *The World Almanac and Book of Facts, 1992* (New York: World Almanac, 1992)

8. *The World Book Encyclopedia*, 21 vols. (Chicago, Toronto, Stuttgart, etc.: Field Enterprises Educational Corporation, 1974)

Appendix 3

EXPANDED BIBLIOGRAPHY OF BOOKS AND OTHER MATERIALS
USEFUL FOR RESEARCHING GERMAN ANCESTORS FROM HUNGARY

A. <u>Books and Research Papers</u>

1. Arbeitsgemeinschaft ostdeutscher Familienforscher e.V. Herne (AGoFF), *Genealogical Guide to German Ancestors from East Germany and Eastern Europe*, 2nd ed., translated by Joachim O. R. Nuthack and Adalbert Goertz (Neustadt/Aisch, Germany: Verlag Degener & Co., 1984; new edition in progress)

2. Arbeitsgemeinschaft ostdeutscher Familienforscher e.V., Herne (compiled be Erich Quester), *Wegweiser für die Forschung nach Vorfahren aus den ostdeutschen und sudetendeutschen Gebieten sowie aus den deutschen Siedlungsgebieten in Ost- und Südosteuropa (AGoFF Wegweiser)*, 3rd ed. (Neustadt/Aisch: Verlag Degener & Co., 1991; new edition in progress)

3. Baxter, Angus, *In Search of Your European Roots* (Baltimore: Genealogical Publishing Co., Inc., 1986)

4. Bellingham, Mary, Edward R. Brandt, Kent Cutkomp and Kermit Frye, *Germanic Genealogy: A Guide to Worldwide Sources and Migration Patterns* (St. Paul: Germanic Genealogy Society, 1995; replaces *Research Guide to German-American Genealogy*)

5. Connor, Martha Remer, *Germans & Hungarians - 1828 Hungarian Land Census* (Author, 7754 Pacement Ct., Las Vegas, NV 89117))
Book # 1: Bács Bodrog County (Batschka) (47,059 names, 110 cities, 450 pp.)
Book # 2: Baranya County (Schwäbische Türkei) (30,975 names, 354 cities, 470 pp.)
Book # 3: Torontal County (Banat) (48,981 names, 160 cities, 553 pp.)
Book # 4: Tolna County (25,461 names, 107+ cities, 285 pp.)
Book # 5: Temes County (189 cities; 568 pp.)
Book # 6: Fejér County (in progress)
Booklet listing the 1828 Hungarian Land Census Cities in the counties in the first 5 books (16 pp.)

6. Genealogical Department of the Church of Jesus Christ of Latter-day Saints, "Records of Genealogical Value for Hungary," Series C, No. 17 (Salt Lake City, 1979)

7. Glazier, Ira A., and William Filby, *Germans to America: Lists of Passengers Arriving at United States Ports* (Wilmington, DE: Scholarly Resources, Inc.); 35 vols.

covering 1850-81 published to date; series is to continue through 1893

8. Jensen, Larry O., "Tracing Germans in Southeast Europe," in *German Genealogical Digest*, Vol. VII, No. 3 (3rd quarter, 1991), pp. 84-91

9. Kathy Karocki, *Tracing Your Hungarian Roots* (Toledo: author, 1993; part of Birmingham Cultural Series)

10. Komjathy, Anthony, and Rebecca Stockell, *German Minorities and the Third Reich* (New York: Holmes and Meier, 1980)

11. Michels, John M., *Introduction to the Hungarian-Germans of North Dakota* (Bismarck, ND: Germans from Russia Heritage Society, February 1988)

12. National Archives Trust Fund Board, *Immigrant and Passenger Arrivals: A Select Catalog of National Archives Microfilm Publications* (Washington, DC, 1983)

13. Puskás, Julianna, *From Hungary to the United States (1880-1914)* (Budapest: Hungarian Academy of Sciences, 1982)

14. Rottenberg, Dan, *Finding Our Fathers: A Guide to Jewish Genealogy* (Baltimore: Genealogical Publishing Co., Inc., 1977, reprinted 1986)

15. *Der Schlüssel* (index to German genealogical periodicals) (Neustadt/Aisch: Heinz-Reise-Verlag, ongoing series)

16. Schenk, Trudy, Ruth Froelke and Inge Bork, *The Wuerttemberg Emigration Index* (Salt Lake City: Ancestry, Inc., 5 vols. to date, ongoing series)

17. Schlyter, Daniel M., *A Handbook of Czechoslovak Genealogy* (Orem, UT: Genun, 1985)

18. Schmidt, Josef, *Die Banater Kirchenbücher* (Stuttgart: Bibliothek und Dokumentationsstelle des Instituts für Auslandsbeziehungen, 1979)

19. Smith, Clifford Neal, and Anna Piszczan-Czaja Smith, *Encyclopedia of German-American Genealogical Research* (New York: R. R. Bowker, 1976)

20. Steigerwald, Jacob, *Tracing Romania's Heterogeneous German Minority from Its Origins to the Diaspora* (Winona, MN: author, 1985)

21. Suess, Jared H., *Central European Genealogical Terminology* (Logan, UT: Everton, 1987)

22. Suess, Jared H., *Handy Guide to Hungarian Genealogical Records* (Logan, UT: Everton Publishers, 1980)

23. Tafferner, Anton, Josef Schmidt, and Josef Volmar Senz, *Danube Swabians in the Pannonia Basin: A New German Ethnic Group* (Milwaukee, 1982)

24. Thode, Ernest, *Address Book for Germanic Genealogy*, 5th ed. (Baltimore: Genealogical Publishing Co., Inc., 1994)

25. Wagner, Ernst, et al, *The Transylvanian Saxons: Historical Highlights* (Cleveland: Alliance of Transylvanian Saxons, 1982)

26. Wermes, Martina, Renate Jude, and Hans-Jürgen Voigt (comp.), *Bestandsverzeichnis der Deutschen Zentralstelle für Genealogie, Leipzig, Teil II: Die archivalischen und Kirchenbuchunterlagen deutscher Siedlungsgebiete im Ausland: Bessarabien, Bukowina, Estland, Lettland und Litauen, Siebenbürgen, Sudetenland, Slowenien und Südtirol* (Neustadt/Aisch, Germany: Verlag Degener & Co., 1992)

27. Wilhelm, Franz, and Josef Kallbrunner, *Quellen zur deutschen Siedlungsgeschichte in Südosteuropa* (Munich, Germany: Verlag von Ernst Reinhardt, 1938)

28. Zimmerman, Gary J., and Marion Wolfert, *German Immigrants: Lists of Passengers Bound from Bremen to New York, with Places of Origin* (Baltimore: Genealogical Publishing Co., Inc., 1988) Vol. 1: 1847-1854; Vol. 2: 1855-1862; Vol. 3: 1863-1867. Series continued by Marion Wolfert: Vol. 4: 1868-71; Vol. 5 being printed.

B. Gazetteers and Atlases

1. Batowski, Henryk, *Słownik Nazw Miejscowych Europy Srodkowej i Wschodniej XIX i XX Wieku* (Warsaw: Państwowe Wydawnictwo Naukowe, 1964) -- a comprehensive gazetteer of Central and East European place names in 24 languages; organized so it can be used even if you don't know Polish

2. János Dvorzák (comp.), *Magyarország Helységnévtára* (Budapest: "Havi Füzetek," 1877)

3. Gardiner, Duncan B., *German Towns in Slovakia & Upper Hungary: A Genealogical Gazetteer*, 3rd ed. (Lakewood, OH: The Family Historian, 1991) -- the authoritative source on this subject

4. Gilbert, Martin, *The Jewish History Atlas* (London, England: Weidenfeld and Nicolson, 1976)

5. Kredel, Otto, and Franz Thierfelder, *Deutsch-fremdsprachiges Ortsnamenverzeichnis* (Berlin: Deutsche Verlagsgesellschaft GmbH, 1931) -- a huge gazetteer, which gives the pre-1914 German place names and the names in other languages when names were changed after World War I following boundary changes

6. Magocsi, Paul Robert, *Historical Atlas of East Central Europe* (Seattle: University of Washington Press, 1993; Vol. I of scheduled 10-volume series, *A History of East Central Europe*)

7. *Ortsverzeichnis der K.K. öster.-ung. Monarchie* (Vienna: K.K. Statistische Zentralkommission, 1915)

8. Pfohl, Ernst, *Ortslexikon Sudetenland* (Nürnberg: Helmut Preußler Verlag, reprinted 1987) -- includes Slovakia, notwithstanding its title

9. Raffelsperger, Franz, *Allgemeines Geographisch-Statistisches Lexikon aller Österreichischen Staaten*, 7 vols. (Vienna: Druck und Verlag der k.k.a.p. typo-geographischen Kunstanstalt, 1845-53)

10. Reichling, Gerhard (ed.), *Gemeindeverzeichnis für die Hauptwohnortgebiete der Deutschen außerhalb der Bundesrepublik Deutschland*, 2nd ed. (Frankfurt am Main: Verlag für Standesamtswesen, 1982)

11. Regényi, Isabella, and Anton Scherer, *Donauschwäbisches Ortsnamenbuch für die ehemals und teilweise noch deutsch besiedelten Orte in Ungarn, Jugoslawien (ohne Slowenien) sowie West-Rumänien* (Darmstadt: 1980)

12. Rohrer, Rudolf M., *Administratives Gemeindelexikon der Čechoslovakischen Republik* (Prague: Statistisches Staatsamt, 1927-28)

13. Rudolph, H., *Vollständigstes geographisch-topographisch-statistisches Orts-Lexikon von Deutschland sowie der unter Österreichs und Preußens Botmäßigkeit stehenden nichtdeutschen Länder* (Weimar: Karl Voigt, Jr., ca. 1861-62) -- a huge work covering all localities under Austrian, Prussian and other German rulers before German unification

14. Scherer, Anton, *Donauschwäbische Bibliographie, 1935-1955* (Munich: Verlag des Südostdeutschen Kulturwerks, 1966)

15. Statistisches Bundesamt and Bundesausgleichsamt, *Gemeindeverzeichnis für Mittel- und Ostdeutschland und die früheren deutschen Siedlungsgebiete im Ausland* (Frankfurt/Main, Germany: Verlag für Standesamtswesen GmbH, 1970) -- official gazetteer of the German government

16. Thode, Ernest, *Atlas for Germanic Genealogy*, 3rd ed. (Marietta, OH: Heritage House, 1988)

17. U. S. Office of Geography, Department of the Interior, *Official Standard Names Approved by the U.S. Board on Geographic Names* (Washington: Government Printing Office; separate volumes for Austria, Hungary, Romania, Yugoslavia and other countries, with periodic updating bulletins to reflect changes)

Table 1

NUMBER OF NATIVE GERMAN-SPEAKERS IN PRE-1914 HUNGARY, BY REGIONS AS DEFINED BY WINKLER, IN ORDER OF SUCH POPULATION IN 1910

Region	Now In	Germans, 1910
Banat[1]	Romania, Serbia[7]	426,240
Burgenland[2]	Hungary, Austria	278,326
Siebenbürgen (Transylvania)	Romania	234,085
Batschka[3]	Hungary, Serbia[7]	190,697
Swabian Turkey[4]	Hungary, Croatia	186,223
North of Lake Balaton[5]	Hungary	172,911
Croatia, Slavonia & Fiume	Croatia	136,393
Slovakia (Zips, Kremnitz & Deutsch-Proben)	Slovakia	94,730
Total[6]		1,719,605

[1] A very tiny portion (3 villages south of the Maros River and east of the Tisza River, near Szeged) extends into Hungary.

[2] Split between Hungary and Austria, but the population figures appear to be those for the Hungarian portion only, since the book which is the source of these figures focuses particularly on Germans in non-Germanic countries.

[3] Straddling the Hungarian-Serbian border, with the Southern Batschka in the Serbian Vojvodina apparently including more Germans in 1910.

[4] Sometimes the term "Swabian Turkey" refers to the northern part of this area, which is in Hungary, and the southern part, with more Germans, split between Hungary and Croatia, as the Baranya region.

[5] This area is sometimes also referred to as the Central Highlands region of Hungary.

[6] Winkler shows a total of 2,037,435 Germans under Hungarian rule. I have been unable to find any reference to the City of Budapest, which is independent of any county, and where a large number of Germans lived, in the Winkler book. According to *Meyers Kleines Konversations-Lexikon*, 9.3% of the people in Budapest in 1906 were Germans, which would amount to about 74,000 people. Winkler also apparently omitted statistics for counties where the number of Germans was very small, since he has no data for the eastern half of present-day Hungary. However, this latter figure could not have been very high, unless the Jews were counted as Germans (as was the case for pre-1867 data), so there is still some uncertainty as to the discrepancy.

[7] These areas are in the Vojvodina, once a semi-autonomous Serbian province in the former federation of Yugoslavia. This area is north of pre-World War I Serbia.

Additional Notes:
(1) A few of the German settlements in Slovakia are now in Carpatho-Ukraine.
(2) Considerably less than half of the ethnic Germans under Hungarian rule before 1914 lived in what is now Hungary. Obviously one is likely to find more information about these people in the Hungarian archives than about those in areas ceded by Hungary after World War I, but some of the Hungarian archives (especially the national and religious archives) include information about the latter as well. Since it has been difficult to get genealogical information from Romania and Yugoslavia until now, the Hungarian archives may offer relatively good prospects for finding information about the very large number of Germans who lived in areas now belonging to those countries. This would be much less applicable to the smaller number who were transferred to the jurisdiction of Austria and Czechoslovakia (excluding the present Carpatho-Ukraine), but even in these cases the Hungarian archives could prove to be a useful secondary source of information.
(3) In 1910 native German-speakers accounted for at least 30% of the total population in Burgenland and Swabian Turkey. The Germans accounted for 20-30% of the people in Zips, Batschka and Banat. They constituted 9.8% of the total population in lands under the Hungarian crown, down from 12.1% in 1890. Much of this decline was undoubtedly accounted for by emigration, but other factors (e.g., changing one's mother tongue from German to Hungarian and possibly differing birth rates) also played a role.

Source of data: Prof. Dr. Wilhelm Winkler, *Statistisches Handbuch des gesamten Deutschtums* (Berlin: Verlag Deutsche Rundschau, 1927), primarily Table 36 on pp. 103-104. The explanatory notes, and any possible errors in them, are the responsibility of the compiler.

Table 2

HUNGARIAN COUNTIES AND CITIES WITH MORE THAN 20,000 NATIVE GERMAN-SPEAKERS IN 1910, EXCLUDING THE AREAS IN SEMI-AUTONOMOUS CROATIA-SLAVONIA NOT IDENTIFIED BY COUNTY BY WINKLER

County	Germans in 1910
Slovakia (with Slovak and Hungarian Names in Parentheses)	
Zips (Spiš, Szepes)	38,434
Neutra (Kremnitz/Deutsch-Proben) (Nitra, Nyitra)	27,937
Burgenland (Western Hungary)	
Wieselburg (now Moson part of Győr-Moson-Sopron)	51,997
Ödenburg, incl. Ödenburg City (now Sopron part of Győr-Moson-Sopron)	109,160
Eisenburg (now Vas, also small part in Slovenia)	117,169
North of Lake Balaton (Central Highlands)	
Veszprém	29,283
Pest-Pilis (now Pest)	83,496
Fejér	23,727
Swabian Turkey	
Tolna (Tolnau)	74,376
Baranya, incl. Fünfkirchen (Pécs) City (now partly in Croatia)	111,847
Batschka	
Bács-Bodrog (now Bács-Kiskun; larger part now in the Vojvodina)	178,950
Banat (now in Romania and Vojvodina)	
Torontal (Romania & Vojvodina, with small part in Hungary)	158,312
Temes (Romania and Vojvodina)	120,683
Arad (Romania, with small part in Hungary)	34,330
Krassó-Szöreny (Romania)	55,883
Siebenbürgen (Transylvania, now in Romania)	
Hermannstadt (Sibiu, Szeben)	49,757
Kleinkokel (Hung.: Kis-Küküllö, northwest of Sibiu)	20,272
Grosskokel (Hung.: Nagy-Küküllö, n.w. of Sibiu)	62,224
Kronstadt (Brașov, Brassó)	29,542
Bistritz-Naszod (Bistrița-Năsăud, Besztercze-Naszód)	25,609
Cities	
Temeschburg/Temeschwar-Josephstadt (Temesvár in Hungarian, now Timișoara, Romania)	31,556

Source of data: Prof. Dr. Wilhelm Winkler, *Statistisches Handbuch des gesamten Deutschtums* (Berlin: Verlag Deutsche Rundschau, 1927), primarily Table 36 on pp. 103-104, but with information on current names and jurisdictions from Tables 6, 6a, 7, 8, 10, 10a, 11, 11a, 12, 12a, 13, 13a, 14, 14a, 15 and 15a on pp. 587-591 and 596-641 of the appendix (*Anhang*), which list in great detail all the communities which once had a German majority and those which once had a German minority. Table 9 deals with the Sathmar (Szatmár, Satu Mare) area, which was divided between Romania and Czechoslovakia, with a tiny portion in Hungary. This area is not listed in Table 36. The compiler also matched the old German county names (Germans use the word "Komitat" for Hungarian counties) and the present-day Hungarian names. Counties straddling the border between Hungary and other countries have new county boundaries now, of course. Boundary changes have also occurred within Hungary itself.

Map 1

HUNGARY BEFORE AND AFTER WORLD WAR I

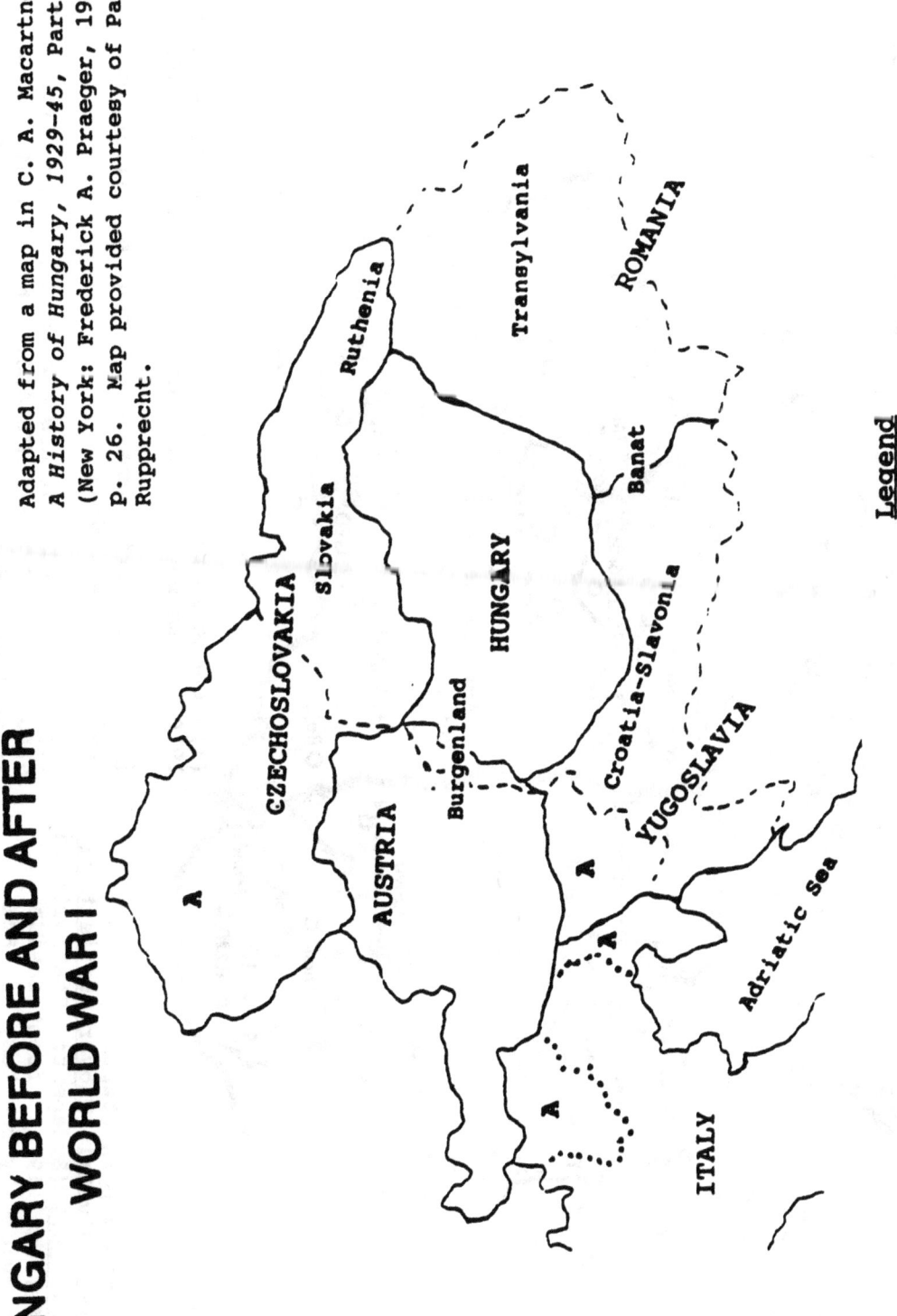

Adapted from a map in C. A. Macartney, *A History of Hungary, 1929-45*, Part I (New York: Frederick A. Praeger, 1956), p. 26. Map provided courtesy of Paul Rupprecht.

Legend

Solid line shows national borders after World War I
Broken line shows boundaries of Hungary before World War I
∧ shows territory ceded by Austria after World War I
Names all in capitals are names of countries after World War I
Names with capitals only at beginning show regions

Map 2

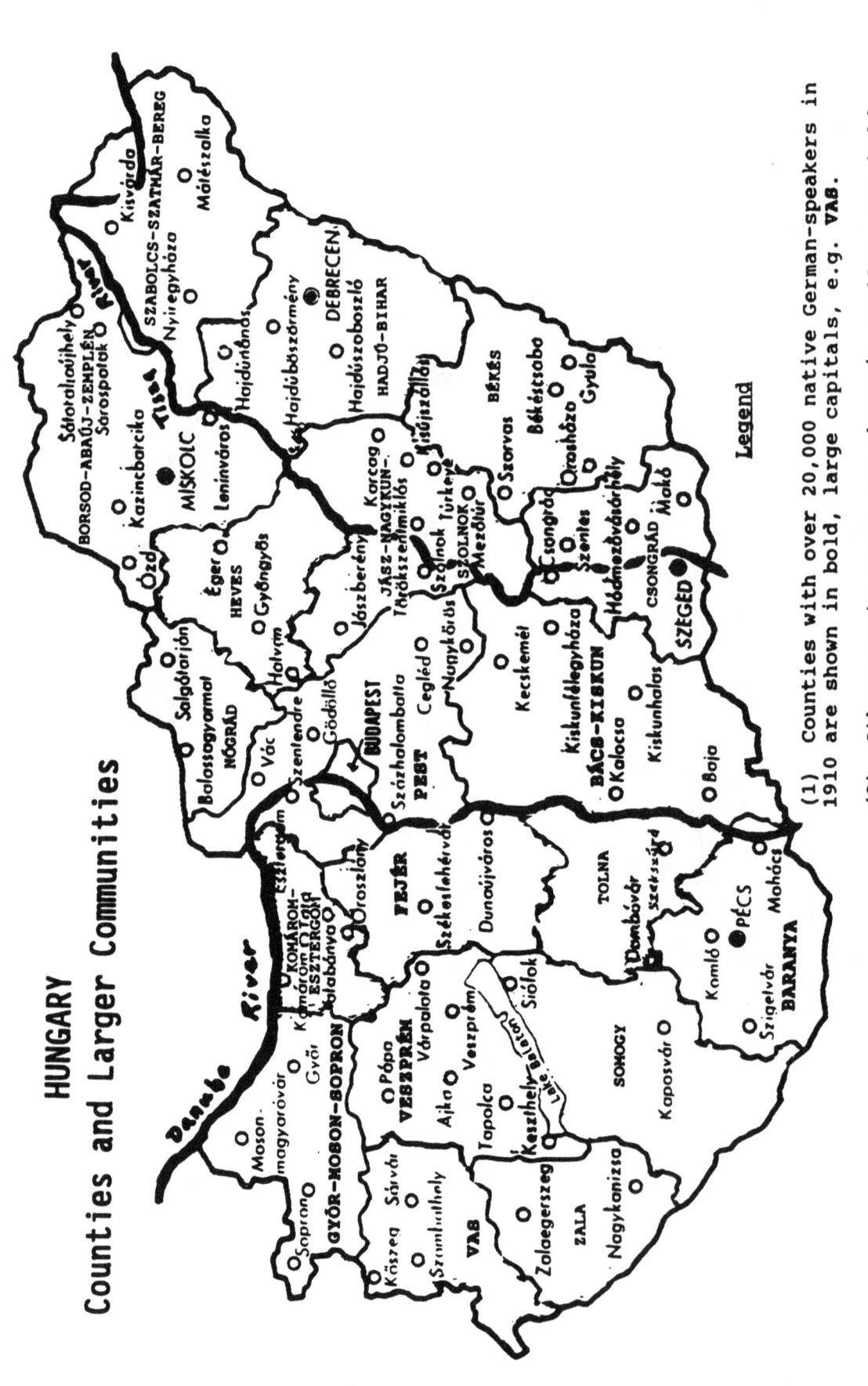

Map 3

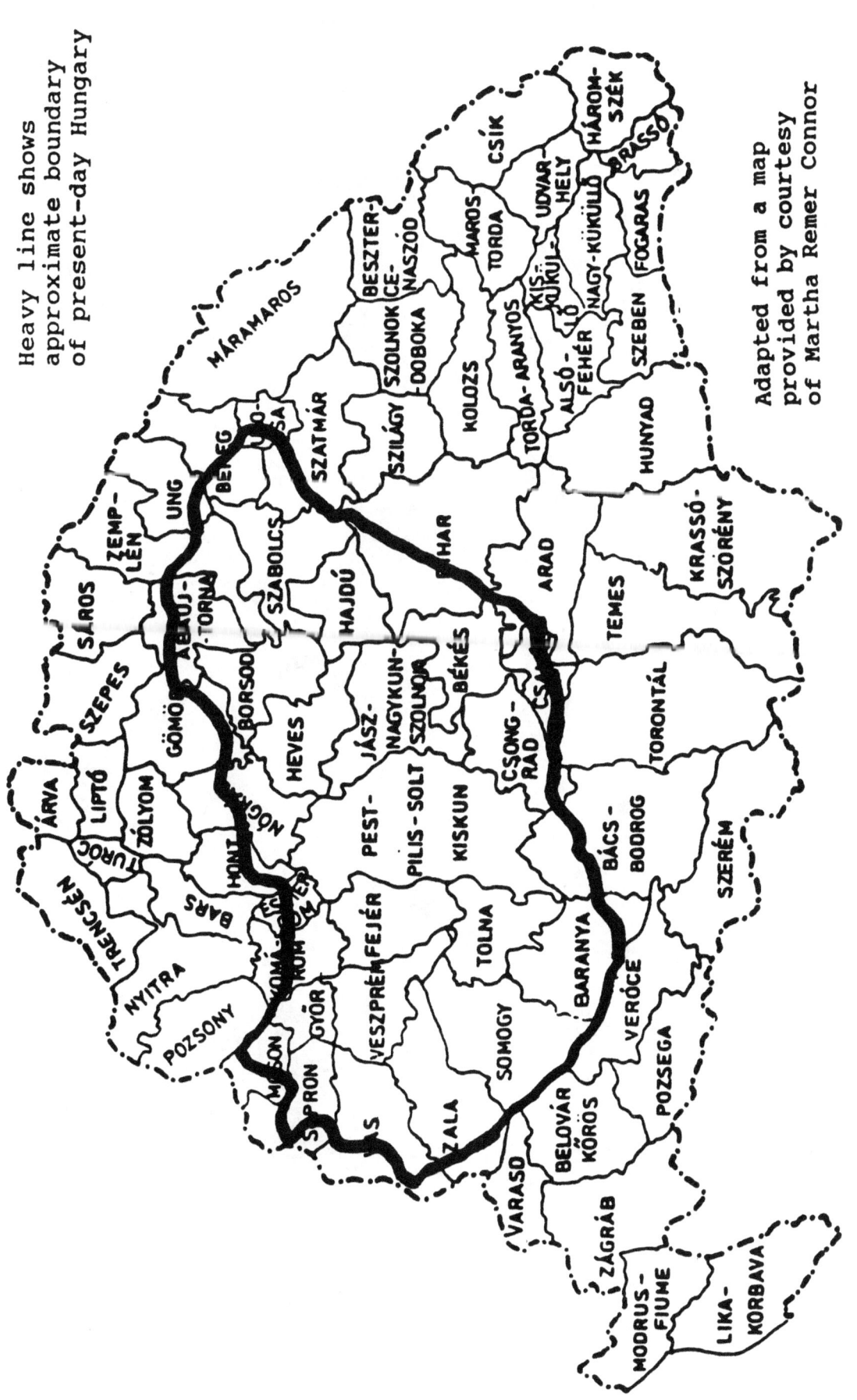

www.ingramcontent.com/pod-product-compliance
Lightning Source LLC
Chambersburg PA
CBHW080252170426
43192CB00014BA/2659